A WOMAN'S SELF-LOVE

Self-Love and Self-Compassion for Women 5 Easy Steps to Transform Your Life by Cultivating Self-Compassion and Overcoming Self-Criticism

VICTORIA BURSHTEIN

CONTENTS

INTRODUCTION: SELF-LOVE AND YOU

According to a cross-cultural study on how gender and age influence self-image (Bleidorn et al., 2016), men tend to have higher levels of self-image compared to women. These results were consistent in each age group and in every country (this study was conducted on 985,000 participants, aged 16 to 45, from 48 different countries). These findings are quite concerning and may prompt you to wonder why women tend to have a lower self-image, self-love, or self-acceptance than men. The answer may lie in the biological sphere (differences in hormones and neurotransmitters) or the cultural sphere (a society's gender norms or beauty standards). Often, it is a mixture of both. Regardless of the cause, the generally low levels of self-esteem in women must be addressed so that they may thrive.

The main goal of this book is to recognize the problem of low self-love in women and tackle this issue head-on. I have personally experienced how self-love can be increased by cultivating self-compassion and addressing self-critical thoughts and beliefs. Once you do this, you will be more willing and able to experience deeper love and stronger connections with yourself, others, and the world around you. Sadly, many women today haven't been taught self-love. It's not a subject you can learn in school or university and often your parents or mentors overlook it. Many societies take self-love for granted—assuming that each individual will learn it by themselves or that it will develop naturally. For example, Western culture emphasizes individualism, and everyone is expected to display a high level of confidence and self-assurance. Such qualities, however, require a genuine sense of self-love which is a hard-won skill that requires lots of practice, patience, and mental strength. The combination of self-love being overlooked and being hard to obtain may result in many women suffering low levels of self-love.

When you do not readily love and accept yourself, you will find yourself on a slippery slope to unhappiness. You will fall prey to excessive self-criticism by always finding faults within yourself and putting yourself down. This creates an unfriendly, unsupportive, and toxic mental environment which will hinder your growth and strain your relationship with yourself and others. This then leads to a sense of disconnection from the world and the self. In this state, your mind suffers as it constantly rejects itself while trying to survive. The disparity between your reality, values, and judgments will also create a lot of distress. You may physically withdraw from the world—afraid that others will see you as you see yourself and thus judge you negatively. Or you may withdraw from the world subconsciously—too caught up in the negativity you've created in your mind. Thus, having low levels of self-love will lead you to take your abilities, your relationships with others, and the beauty of the world around you for granted.

On another note, if you do not possess self-love, you may feel like you're not enough and search for joy and contentment outside of yourself. Without self-love, you will always be criticizing yourself and this may lead you to overemphasize your flaws while idolizing others. This can guide you to falsely believe that you're never good enough. For example, if you place second in a competition, you can only focus on the one person who beat you as opposed to your achievement. If someone compliments you, you shrug it off and pay attention to your flaws to negate what they've said. This mindset will chip away at your self-worth and cause a lot of stress and sadness. To compensate for these negative emotions, you may lose yourself by constantly searching for joy elsewhere. While you may take better care of your physical health, strive to achieve greater things, enter into romantic relationships, or shop online, without a healthy level of self-love, your happiness will be suboptimal and fleeting. This is because the first step to being happy with your life is to be happy with yourself. It is from this seed that other fruits may spring.

If you are a woman who relates to the descriptions above, then you need to start focusing on cultivating self-love. Reading this book is a great first step. This book will demonstrate how to develop and strengthen not only your self-love but also your self-awareness and passion for living. As stated, self-love is vital for your general happiness, and equally as important is your self-awareness which can help you take stock of your beliefs, assumptions, and values. By practicing self-awareness daily, you will notice that you can live a more purposeful, guided, and insightful life. When you're more cognizant of your thoughts and feelings, you begin to shape your life and live according to your values. A joy for life will invariably come once you've developed your self-love and self-awareness as you will be more open to the possibilities and beauties of life.

Below is an outline of the chapters of this book so that you know what to expect with each section as you organize your thoughts and prepare yourself for what you will learn.

In Chapter 1, you will learn about self-criticism and the differences between destructive and constructive criticism. Criticism isn't always bad as it can be helpful and insightful. More often than not, however, the critic inside your head may be unhelpful, unwanted, and unnecessarily hurtful. To address your inner critic and better guide it to help you, you must understand how healthy criticism can foster growth.

In Chapter 2, you will study the key to self-love: self-compassion. You will learn about the benefits of self-compassion and its three components that will aid you on your journey to self-love. These components are self-kindness, mindfulness, and common humanity.

In Chapter 3, you will explore the different masks of self-compassion that often confuse people. These masks include self-pity, self-indulgence, and self-esteem. Self-pity and self-indulgence are pernicious masks that will damage your mental health if you continue to mistake them for self-compassion. On the other hand, self-esteem is a healthy trait but still one that shouldn't be mistaken for self-compassion. The two may interlink in their effects but they remain fundamentally separate concepts.

In Chapter 4, you will start to learn about the LOVE system and the first of five steps in developing your self-love: embracing your self-critic. There are huge differences between destructive self-criticism and self-reflection. This chapter will help you switch your inner critic from harshly criticizing you to constructively providing you with feedback and insightful reflections.

In Chapter 5, you will enter the second of the five steps and the "L" in the LOVE system: Luring the voice in your head with compassion. You will be given several practices to improve your self-compassion which will help you silence the negative criticism in your mind.

In Chapter 6, you will move on to the third step and the "O" in the LOVE system: Obsessing over loving and accepting yourself. In this chapter, you will learn how to love and accept every part of yourself including your strengths, flaws, and personality.

In Chapter 7, you will land on the fourth step and the "V" in the LOVE system: Viewing others through the eyes of love and compassion. Self-love is crucial to strengthening your bond with others. When you love yourself, you will have more affection, patience, and compassion to offer to others.

In Chapter 8, you will study the fifth and final step and the "E" in the LOVE system: Embracing the world. You will discover how to better interact with the world in this chapter using worksheets that will train you to view the world through love and compassion.

My Story

I sincerely hope that you can receive and benefit from all the advice provided in this book and create your own path towards self-love. This topic hits close to home for me as I struggled with self-love for much longer than I care to admit. Growing up, I was fortunate enough to be blessed with many advantages. I was born and raised in East Europe, surrounded by a loving family, and then I moved to New York City in my early 20s. I was able to graduate with a degree in Business and Administration and land a dream job in financial services. I even had the financial and emotional support to pursue and obtain my Masters in Marketing and Management. I've also been endlessly blessed in other areas of my life. I'm currently married with two wonderful children and my everyday life allows me to pursue many of my hobbies, such as writing, reading, fitness, traveling, art, architecture and history. I say all this not to brag or to give you the false impression that my life has always been perfect. It's to highlight that, even with all my blessings (which I was and am enormously grateful for), I found that I was still lacking joy and contentment for a long time.

I couldn't find any external reason for my discontentment, so I eventually realized that my thoughts and my mind were making me unhappy. Once I recognized my problem (a dire lack of self-love and self-compassion), I began my journey of self-improvement. This was a constant uphill battle, especially as my inner critic had become so loud and incessant over the years. I had to relearn how to think and approach myself, and gradually I became better at being kind to myself. I also concurrently became more compassionate to those around me. All in all, I gained a lot from my struggle to develop self-love and I would like to share these benefits with others who are going through the same pain.

Helping you achieve self-love through the contents of this book matters deeply to me so I've included all the exercises and information that helped me love myself more and see myself, others, and the world around me through a loving and joyful perspective. I believe that I can offer helpful solutions for women suffering from low self-love as I have a passion for self-improvement and solidarity with women. I simply want to help all women achieve happiness and experience life to the fullest. Without further delay, let's dive right into the process of self-improvement!

CHAPTER 1

DESTRUCTIVE
OR
CONSTRUCTIVE
CRITICISM

A lack of self-love is an epidemic among women across the globe. One of the main reasons for this is the way you speak to yourself. Everyone has conversations with themselves that help them make sense of the world, so the tone and content of these conversations have a big effect on your mental health, perceptions, and general wellbeing. As a woman, your inner conversations may veer more toward negative or destructive criticism as you pick on your flaws, insult yourself, degrade your worth, or minimize your achievements. Such conversations can harm your levels of self-love and make you feel disconnected from yourself and others. If you always indulge in negative or destructive self-criticism, you will always see the bad side of things and you will have very little confidence. In this chapter, you will learn to understand and control your inner critic by exploring the origins and downsides of destructive criticism while discovering the characteristics and benefits of constructive criticism.

In Chapter 4, you will learn about the need for criticism in more detail. For now, it's enough to say that self-criticism can help you become more self-aware. When done properly, self-criticism will alert you to what you can improve and remind you to keep working on yourself. This can positively affect your self-esteem and help you become a more well-rounded individual as you constantly strengthen your good points, address your weak points, and adapt your behavior. This form of self-criticism can be called constructive criticism. On the other end of the spectrum is destructive criticism which is wholly unhelpful and unhealthy.

The Characteristics, Origins, and Harms of Destructive Criticism

What Is Self-Criticism?

Self-criticism in its destructive manifestation can be understood as your tendency to evaluate and judge yourself too harshly without plans to grow and improve. You may endlessly scrutinize or nitpick your performance, thoughts, actions, and personality to tell yourself that you're currently not good enough and will never be good enough. Being self-critical is a common personality trait which means that it falls on a spectrum for everyone. Some people may be harder on themselves than others. These same people may be more inclined to concentrate on the negative side of things because destructive criticism leaves no room for a silver lining. This is a wholly pessimistic perspective that concentrates all your energy and attention on what's wrong in your life. Destructive criticism thus distracts you from future positive experiences by causing your thoughts to spiral into harmful tangents of self-doubt, self-hate, and isolation.

Another characteristic of destructive criticism is that it's completely unhelpful. It offers you no way forward to improve your flaws. Rather, it simply judges you or labels you negatively. Even if your destructive self-criticism does come up with a possible solution, this solution will be negated by more destructive self-criticism that tells you that you're incapable of seeing that solution through.

Some examples of destructive criticism are thoughts such as: "I'm so stupid," "I'm a failure," "I can't do anything right," "Even if I try, I'll only fail," "Why didn't I do better on that test?" and "I don't deserve love and kindness." You can see the characteristics of destructive criticism listed in these examples. They are too harsh, overly focused on the

negative side of things, and absolute—providing no possibility of a silver lining or alternative. Clearly, these examples are completely unhelpful to your self-development as
they offer only judgments and no way to better yourself.
Understanding the characteristics of destructive criticism
is the first step to recognizing when you're being overly
critical toward yourself and hindering growth. Once you
recognize these habits, you will be able to change them.

Potential Origins

Just as importantly, you must understand the origins of destructive criticism. This can help you be more understanding toward yourself. Rather than falling into the self-defeating cycle of criticizing yourself for being too critical,
understanding how you learned to be this way can mitigate
feelings of shame and guilt. Being destructively critical of
yourself doesn't mean that you're weaker or less reasonable
than others, it simply means that there were factors in your
life that led you to think this way. As you read through the
possible origins of destructive criticism, try to reflect on
your history to see if any of these origins apply to you. It's
always comforting to have a better understanding of what
could have possibly caused you to develop certain habits
or thought patterns. At the same time, remember to affirm
to yourself that it's not important whose fault it is that you
think this way. You're not gaining information right now to
assign blame. You're on this journey to improve yourself
and foster self-love. What's most important is accepting
that this is how you think currently and you must now find

a way to overcome these thoughts. Your past may have caused your destructive criticism but your present is what's maintaining it. One possible origin of destructive criticism may be your early relationships with your family or mentors. If your parents had high expectations and goals for you, then you may have felt pressured to achieve more and you may have judged yourself when you fell short of these objectives. If you had a sibling who excelled in school, beat you in most sports, or received more attention and praise, then you may have been pushed to compare yourself to them and easily believed that you were no good.

Observing how others criticized themselves may also have cultivated your destructive criticism. For example, if you often observed your loved ones being overly critical of their achievements or talents, you likely took this as guidance for how you should be. Thus, in childhood, you began to mimic this behavior until it became a habit.

Observing how others treated you may have also influenced your development of destructive criticism. For example, if your parents openly expressed their high expectations of others and subsequent disappointments to you, this may have made you even more inclined to negatively assess yourself to extreme levels. If others criticized you harshly, you may have internalized that criticism and come to believe that they were right.

Another possible origin is your religion or culture. If these parts of your life instill high demands on yourself and constantly remind you that you're not good enough, then you will be more likely to develop destructive criticism. Your culture may devalue you or your religious teachers may wrongly preach to you that you're not enough. Whatever it is, you will feel small, insignificant, and inherently bad. This will then cause you to criticize yourself too harshly.

Unhealthy relationships can also fuel your destructive criticism. If your friends or partners undermine you, constantly insult you, or blame you for their failures, then you may start to believe that you're worthless, that you're always in the wrong, that you're ugly or stupid, and so on. You will eventually feel fundamentally flawed, undesirable, and unworthy of love, which will spark more destructive criticism.

Next, you may have developed destructive criticism because you believe tough love will push you to do better. Many cultures advocate the importance of being the best and many people misunderstand that being harsh and hard with themselves will motivate them to perform better. You may even believe that if you're not hard on yourself then you will become a lazy, worthless, and unproductive person; however, this is completely untrue. While tough love may be useful to push yourself and not accept lame excuses from yourself, it's vital to understand that tough love never entails destructive criticism. Tough love entails forcing yourself to confront challenges for self-improvement, pushing yourself within your limits, and knowing when you're too worn out to go on or when you're using excuses to slack off. Destructive criticism does none of this as it only makes you feel bad about yourself and tries to push you regardless of your realistic limitations. So, while tough love involves holding yourself to high standards and achieving realistic goals, destructive criticism breaks you down and demotivates you.

Many people may fall into destructive criticism when they mistake it for modesty. Have you ever replied to a compliment with a self-deprecating joke? Perhaps you fear that accepting the compliment is a form of arrogance and you believe that insulting yourself will ensure you stay humble. Rather than appearing vain or boastful, you'd rather beat yourself up. This habit may stem from your old, childhood ways of viewing humility and pride; however, you can't control how others view you. You can only live according to your values, and how others judge you is their business. If you truly believe that destructive criticism is a form of humility and that accepting compliments is a form of arrogance, try to remind yourself that humility involves having a realistic view of yourself. To be humble, you must be aware of your strengths and weaknesses. So, if the compliment applies, then gracefully accept it. There is more humility in accepting a compliment than rejecting one that is true. Accepting the compliment could also give you insight into your positive qualities and others will be happy to have made you smile and feel appreciated.

The last possible origin is based on a similar misunderstanding: Some people mistake self-compassion for self-indulgence. Self-compassion is the antidote to self-criticism,
but many people are hesitant to practice self-compassion
as they believe that it will make them too soft. Self-compassion can be easily misunderstood as a way of life that
doesn't hold the individual responsible for anything and
doesn't motivate the individual to achieve anything. This
is an erroneous understanding as self-compassion functions in a much more nuanced way that will help you func-
tion optimally and achieve more than you would have if
you were still steeped in destructive criticism. More on
self-compassion will be explored in the next chapter.

The Consequences

One negative consequence of destructive criticism is that
it can fuel your anger toward yourself. This inward anger
may later combine with other negative emotions such as
disgust and self-hatred and may be pointed at some part
of your personality, a choice, or your being as a whole.
As long as you keep destructively criticizing yourself, you
will continue to justify this anger. Long-term anger can be
dangerous and wreak serious havoc on your physical and
emotional health.

Other emotions that are encouraged by your destructive
criticism are guilt and shame. Your sense of guilt will be
increased as you blame yourself for anything and every-

thing going wrong—even if the situation was out of your control. Your sense of shame will also be heightened as you will see yourself as worse than others and unworthy of love. You will feel embarrassed about yourself and ashamed that you're not as good as you want to be.

Another detrimental effect of destructive criticism is how it affects your brain's structure and functioning. The anger that fuels your destructive criticism may be construed by your brain as a threat and this may cause harmful emotional distress. Prolonged distress may then affect your resilience to intense emotions, thus forming an endless cycle of suffering. The three areas of your brain that are most likely to be altered by incessant destructive criticism are your amygdala, hippocampus, and ventromedial prefrontal cortex. These three structures play important roles in regulating your emotions and thoughts. This is how they are affected by destructive criticism:

- The amygdala helps you process your emotions and is linked with your fear responses. When there is more activity in the amygdala (when your destructive criticism raises your brain's alarms), you may become more sensitive and fearful of possible threats regardless of whether the threat is real. This may make you more susceptible to destructive criticism and make you more anxious and fearful.

- The hippocampus is involved with your memory and when it's affected by trauma it will find it more difficult to separate past and present stimuli. For example, if your parents used to scold you harshly, this may have altered the structure of your hippocampus. This would make it harder for your brain to separate past and present experiences and pain when you are criticized as an adult. So, now, you will be quick to assume that an authority figure is displeased with you or disappointed in you. This will feed your destructive criticism as you falsely believe that others also think that you're not good enough.

- The ventromedial prefrontal cortex helps regulate the emotional responses that your amygdala generates, especially your fear responses or responses to threats. When this structure is impaired, you will be less able to regulate these responses appropriately and you will be more sensitive to feeling threatened and afraid.

Other than changes to your brain, destructive criticism also affects the hormones and neurotransmitters in your body. Since criticism may make you feel threatened, your body may engage in its fear response by releasing cortisol. High levels of this hormone for prolonged periods may cause anxiety, fatigue, headaches, and an increased heart rate. Your fear response will also raise your norepinephrine levels which will increase your heart rate and blood pressure. All this will be even more detrimental to you if you're susceptible to stress and can cause you to develop a chronic mental illness such as depression or anxiety.

The Characteristics and Benefits of Constructive Criticism

Sadly, receiving and generating constructive criticism isn't something that comes naturally to people. You need to consciously cultivate it and practice this skill, unlike destructive criticism which is easily picked up and cemented as a habit. The first step in developing constructive criticism is knowing what you're trying to develop. You must understand what constructive criticism looks and feels like to know what you should aim for. So, here are a few basic characteristics of this type of useful criticism.

Firstly, constructive criticism is specific rather than general. Giving yourself specific feedback will provide you with more information on what you need to focus on and what can be done to improve. This makes it easier for you to address the criticism. For example, destructive criticism may say, "I need to be smarter and do better in my exams." This is a general statement that offers you no road forward. Constructive criticism would say, "I need to become more familiar with calculus and biology." Specifying which sections you must focus on provides you with a clear goal and allows you to start imagining what actions can be taken to meet that goal.

Next, constructive criticism is supportive rather than demeaning. Your criticisms will explain exactly where and why you went wrong while also trying to figure out how you can avoid such mistakes in the future. Rather than passing judgment on what has happened, the constructive critic tries to understand so that you can learn from failure. Destructive criticism may say, "I failed because I'm stupid," passing judgment and lowering your self-worth. In contrast, constructive criticism may say, "I finished my project in haste and didn't have time to check it for errors, so that's why I did poorly." This way, you describe exactly what happened to cause your setback without negatively assessing yourself so that you can learn from your mistakes.

On that note, constructive criticism tackles an issue, rather than you as a person. If you tackle an issue as an external problem, you will feel more capable of fixing it. You will thus approach the issue more objectively and reinforce the idea that you can overcome your problems as long as you work on them. If you attack yourself, you create an unproductive mindset within yourself that you are inherently bad at this task or that there's no way you can solve the issue. For example, destructive feedback may say, "I'm not a good leader so I won't get run in the election." This relates the issue to your personality which is harder to change, and so you will be less willing to believe that you can overcome your problem. Constructive criticism would say, "Speaking in public is hard for me so I need to practice more." While the issue still has to do with you, it is less a judgment on your personality and more an assessment of your weaker points. This way, you can acknowledge that you must work to improve a certain point rather than passing judgment on a fundamental part of yourself.

Similarly, constructive criticism focuses on your behavior rather than on you. Rather than criticizing yourself and negatively labeling yourself because of a certain trait, constructive criticism breaks down the trait into actions, making it more realistic for you to change. Destructive criticism may say, "I'm such a noisy person," asserting a fixed personality trait that feels harder to change. Constructive criticism would say, "I tend to talk over others during social gatherings." This allows for the possibility of change as you can now focus on a specific habit that you want to alter.

Remember that constructive criticism is directed toward things that you can realistically change. If you criticize yourself over something that you can't control, you will only feel powerless, helpless, and frustrated. For example, destructive criticism may say, "I'm ugly because I'm so short" or "I'm ugly because I'm so tall." Since this is something over which you have no control, it's pointless and utterly unhelpful for you to criticize yourself over it.

Moreover, constructive criticism will recognize that you made a mistake but it won't define you by that one error. Destructive criticism may say, "I said something to hurt my mother so I'm a terrible child." This catastrophizes a single mistake and makes you feel terrible about it and as if that one mistake is eternally damning. This may even prevent you from actually addressing your mistake as your attention is pulled inward and you become overly focused on your negative self-assessments. Constructive criticism acknowledges the mistake but focuses on making amends rather than judging yourself. For example, you may think, "I said something to hurt my mother so in the future, I need to be more careful with my words" or "I said something to hurt my mother so I should apologize." Unlike destructive criticism which only offers damning judgments, constructive criticism makes you confront your mistakes and make amends.

Constructive criticism is also a prolonged conversation with yourself. The whole point of this criticism is to improve yourself, and self-improvement takes time, so don't forget to follow up on your criticisms. Since this form of feedback usually leads to solutions that address your weaknesses, be sure to see those solutions through and reassess yourself later on. You can even write down some of your criticisms so that you can track how you're progressing in those areas and gradually transform your weaknesses into strengths. Make sure that you can track your progress in a tangible way. For example, if you wish to work on your patience, turn that into a measurable goal by noting each time you listened to someone without interrupting them.

On the topic of having conversations, a positive characteristic of constructive criticism is that it opens the door to self-awareness. A part of constructive criticism is living according to your values and beliefs, and to do this you will have to reflect and discover what they are. Since constructive criticism pushes you to discover your capabilities and limits, you end up practicing the skill of searching within yourself. With all the self-reflection that goes into constructive criticism, your self-awareness will definitely be heightened.

Furthermore, constructive criticism may focus on others more than destructive criticism does. While destructive criticism pulls your attention inward and causes you to withdraw from the world, constructive criticism may shift your focus to your impact on others and may lead you to consider how your actions can help those around you. This may help you be more engaged in your relationships, less self-centered, and more considerate of others.

Finally, one of the most important characteristics of constructive criticism is that it comes from a healthy place. The main motivations of constructive criticism are a sincere desire to improve yourself and genuine concern for your wellbeing. On the flip side, destructive criticism often comes from a place of self-hatred and anger. When you're trying to distinguish between the two, a useful indicator is to reflect on whether your criticism is coming from concern or anger. Often, your body will give you clues about this such as an elevated heart rate or a sinking feeling in your chest.

The Benefits

Now that you're well versed in the characteristics of constructive criticism, you will be better able to guide your inner critic to be more helpful to you. Just as important is learning about the benefits of constructive criticism so that you're aware of how this form of criticism can help you.

Firstly, constructive criticism can open your eyes to the areas in your life that need improving. In life, everyone needs a balance of confidence, humility, realistic self-perception, and an acknowledgment of their weaknesses. With destructive criticism, you view yourself too negatively and this may demotivate you. Without any criticism at all, you may become apathetic and passive in your own life. A healthy middle ground is where constructive criticism thrives and allows you to recognize your flaws without beating yourself up over them and pushing yourself to do your best while keeping your limitations in mind. Constructive criticism gives you the chance to reflect on your strengths and weaknesses, instilling you with the confidence and courage to address your shortcomings. In doing this, constructive criticism opens you up to various opportunities. As you will constantly be improving yourself, you will find yourself ready and able to handle anything that comes your way. You will also have the mental fortitude and bravery to face new things and try your best in all your endeavors.

On a related note, constructive criticism can help you take realistic, feasible steps toward realizing your full potential. As you previously learned, constructive criticism is based on tackling external issues that are within your control. Rather than obsessing over things you can't change or feeling defeated and helpless, constructive criticism helps you feel in control of your situation. So constructive criticism will help you envision a realistic and optimal version of yourself and then guide you to achieve it.

Another benefit of constructive criticism is that you will have a firm understanding of your strengths and weaknesses. Constructive criticism not only informs you of what areas you can improve on, but it also takes into account your strengths and the full extent of your capabilities so that you know how hard to push yourself and what goals are realistic or not. This will help you be more rational and reasonable with your constructive criticism, and your self-knowledge will also increase. A side effect of this is that you will be able to handle criticism from others more easily. When you reflect on your strengths and weaknesses, then the words of others become less condemning and more insightful or helpful if they come from a sincere place. Sometimes, people may criticize you to tear you down. Other times, people may criticize you from a place of concern to help you. Regardless of their intentions, with a good knowledge of your strengths and weaknesses, you will be able to politely disagree with them, brush off their mean comments, agree with them, or graciously accept their comments and reflect on them later.

You will also be more grounded and resilient as you realize that you're not perfect and that you shouldn't aim to be perfect. You will be able to accept that some things are out of your control and that you live in an inherently chaotic and imperfect world. This acceptance will then make you a more stable person, less affected by the things happening around you, and more at peace with who you are.

So far, you've learned how to identify destructive criticism, how you may have developed it, and its harmful effects, along with constructive criticism, its characteristics, and its benefits. This knowledge will help you pinpoint your harmful thought patterns and replace them with productive thoughts. Remember that criticism isn't inherently bad, it's the type of criticism you participate in that makes a difference. Now that you're more aware of the two types of criticism—a big hurdle on the path to self-love—you will learn about the key to self-love: self-compassion.

CHAPTER 2

SELF-COMPASSION AS THE KEY TO SELF-LOVE

If you imagine self-love as an open field with flowers and sunlight, destructive criticism is the wall that blocks your path, and self-compassion is the ladder you must use to scale that wall. This is to say that self-compassion will lead you to the worthwhile destination of self-love. In this chapter, you will learn about the benefits of self-compassion and its main components. Understanding the benefits of self-compassion may help you reject any misconceptions or excuses that you may use to disregard self-compassion. Many people are initially hesitant to practice this skill, but once you realize the extensive improvements that self-compassion can make in your life, you may become more willing to try it out. Understanding the components of self-compassion is also important as this will help you cultivate it efficiently in yourself. Wanting and choosing to practice self-compassion is only the first step. Like any worthwhile endeavor, you must put in the work, time, and effort to understand it and build it up. By breaking down self-compassion into several components, it will be easier for you to understand this concept and put it into practice.

Self-compassion entails treating yourself like you would treat a friend that you love and care for. Doing so will make you more mindful and more understanding of your situation and its challenges. When faced with mistakes, you will be more gentle with yourself, experience fewer negative emotions, and recognize that failure is an inescapable part of life. This mindset, gained through self-compassion, will help you be stronger and more successful in the future. Constructive criticism, which you explored in the previous chapter, will also come into play as self-compassion is difficult to cultivate if you're entrenched in your destructive criticism.

In the previous chapter, you learned how destructive criticism feeds your negative emotions, makes your mind feel threatened, and initiates your fear responses. All this forms a vicious cycle that perpetuates your destructive criticism and heightens your sensitivity to negative emotions. Your destructive criticism also demonstrates to others that it is ok to treat you poorly. If those around you always observe how you talk down to yourself or insult yourself, then this may become an acceptable norm for them and they may exhibit similar behavior toward you. While others may not actually be trying to harm you; it's a behavior that they could subconsciously have picked up from you. In this way, destructive criticism is like an infectious virus. You may have learned such behavior from your parents or your surroundings, and others may be learning it from you through observation. Unfortunately, bad habits are often easier to pick up than good habits.

If you keep criticizing yourself so harshly and excessively, then the road to self-love will always be blocked as you will never be able to accept yourself or be kind to yourself. Self-compassion paves the way for you to get to self-love by breaking the cycle of destructive criticism. This will be harder for some than others as your inner critic may have already been solidified within you. Bad habits are hard to change, but it's never impossible. You simply need to value yourself enough to put the work in.

The good news is that you can learn to cultivate self-compassion to achieve self-love by yourself. All you need is proper information and the right tools to put you on the right path. So, let's quickly gather all the knowledge you'll need to boost your self-compassion!

Benefits of Self-Compassion

Understanding the benefits of self-compassion will ensure
that you're more motivated to develop this skill and can
help silence all of your misconceptions and excuses that
have kept you from practicing it. The first and most obvious benefit of self-compassion is that it can help you
silence your destructive criticism. By training your mind to
react to situations with more resilience and understanding
you will slowly gear your mind toward useful and positive
factors rather than getting stuck in unhelpful, incessant
negativity. As you studied in the previous chapter, destructive criticism has negative effects on your brain and body.
You will be physically and mentally distressed by your negative thoughts. Self-compassion flips that around by activat-
ing your body's soothing system and biological nurturance.
Rather than triggering your fear responses or making you
feel threatened, self-compassion will encourage your body
to take better care of your mind during times of stress by
producing greater feelings of wellbeing.

Productivity

Self-compassion can also boost productivity. Some people, when faced with failure, will fall into despair and pro-
crastination; however, someone with self-compassion will
understand that failure is not the end but rather a learning
opportunity. Failure is not absolute or final—it's simply a
chance for you to reflect on where you could do better

and try your best next time. So rather than beating yourself up or projecting the one failure into a horrible future for yourself, you will be able to remain calm, assess the situation rationally, and improve yourself. This will maintain your peace of mind which will increase your productivity and chances of success. When you're too busy with your negative thoughts and worries, you will shut down and you won't be able to work or do anything helpful for yourself or your future. If instead, you busy yourself with self-compassion, you will be able to take positive action and keep your mind clear and steady as you keep working. And working to improve yourself will always increase your chances of success as compared to if you were only beating yourself up and indulging in your negative thoughts.

Resilience

Related to this, self-compassion increases your resilience in the face of failure, mistakes, or rejection. Since you will be able to respond to failure productively, you will be able to adapt and handle failure better. Even if you fail, you will get right back up and keep trying. Some overly self-critical people may have a deep aversion to failure and anything that may make them look bad. These people may give up as soon as they face a challenge as they are afraid of failing; however, if you have self-compassion, you will have a mindset that allows for failure as you understand that failure isn't devastating. Consequently, you will be open to more learning experiences.

Self-Worth

Another benefit of self-compassion is that it increases
your self-worth. While destructive criticism is always tear-
ing you down and decreasing your value based on your performance, achievements, or personality, self-compassion
will remind you to value yourself and not make that value
dependent on external factors. A part of self-compassion
is believing that everyone has intrinsic worth, including
yourself. So, even if you mess up or if you don't achieve
as much as you wanted, none of this detracts from your
worth. When you hold onto an innate sense of self-worth,
you will be able to treat yourself more kindly and view
your situations more objectively. You won't be overly affected by setbacks or daunting challenges as you know that
no matter what happens, your sense of worth is protected.
This will allow you to work and improve yourself with less
stress. In tandem with this benefit, self-compassion will
also improve your body image. Some people may be overly
negative toward their bodies as they hinge their self-worth
upon their looks. When you have self-compassion, you will
understand that your body doesn't define your worth and
so you will be able to work to get fitter without stressing
about your self-worth. You will also be more understanding toward yourself as a unique individual with your own
challenges. For example, you may take into account your
body type (there are three main body types, each with a
different rate at which it gains and loses weight) and thus
be more patient with your fitness goals.

One thing to note is that, while self-compassion will prevent you from being too hard on yourself, it definitely doesn't mean that self-compassion will cause you to be too lenient with yourself. Self-compassion doesn't erase your deeper values and goals. It simply helps you be more realistic, reasonable, and kind in your pursuit of those things. It may also help you tweak your goals to make them more rational and healthy. In fact, self-compassion will help you reach your goals more efficiently as you will be more productive and resilient in your pursuits. Now that you understand the various benefits of self-compassion, I hope that you understand how it is a vitally important tool on your journey to self-love and that you won't hesitate to begin cultivating this trait in your life. To help you with this, let's now delve into the three components that make up self-compassion.

The Three Components of Self-Compassion

Self-compassion occurs when you acknowledge your own suffering, flaws, and failures, and choose to respond with understanding, kindness, and care rather than judgment, negativity, or evaluation. This is how you would treat a friend. You would tell them that their failures are part of being human and that they can always work to improve themselves in the future. Just apply all that to yourself and you've got self-compassion! Unfortunately, that's a lot easier said than done. So, let's break it down and see how you can more effectively develop self-compassion. There are three components that you need to focus on:

- Self-kindness: This is where you become aware of your negative inner critic and strive to replace that voice with one that is kinder and more gentle. The opposite of self-kindness is self-judgment—where you constantly put yourself down and devalue yourself. Through self-kindness, you will be able to avoid judging yourself too harshly based on unrealistic expectations. You will also become more accepting of whatever situation you're faced with.

- Mindfulness: This is where you observe your negative emotions but you do not react, emphasize, or suppress them. The opposite of mindfulness is over-identification with your thoughts or emotions. This is where you exaggerate the significance and meaning of your thoughts or emotions. For example, if you're feeling angry, you may think that your anger means that you're a bad person. If you're feeling afraid without any tangible reason, you may think that there's a real threat somewhere. With mindfulness, however, you avoid ruminating on your problems, negative emotions, or troubling thoughts. Such habits are unhelpful, harmful to your mental health, and not conducive to self-improvement. Over-identification with your thoughts and emotions is a destructive thought process that will only hinder your growth and limit your potential. In contrast, mindfulness will help you accept your thoughts and emotions as they come and go, without attaching too much meaning or significance to them. This can increase your self-acceptance and decrease your emotional distress.

- Common humanity: This is where you acknowledge how suffering and failure are common experiences and an inevitable part of being human. The opposite of common humanity is isolation where you remove yourself from the context of the wider human race and view yourself and your experiences in an isolated, singular bubble. For example, when you fail at something, you may then believe that your failure demeans your worth and value. You don't consider how many other people have failed at the same thing and those failures didn't devalue them or stop them from going on to succeed. When you practice common humanity, you will stop seeing yourself from a defeatist, victimized, or narcissistic perspective.

Having broken it down a bit more, you should now have a clearer understanding of the attitudes and mindsets that make up self-compassion. Since self-compassion is such an important tool to help you achieve self-love, let's dive even deeper so that you can more effectively develop this skill.

Self-Kindness

First off, let's explore self-kindness more. What attitudes, feelings, actions, and words come to mind when you think of someone being kind? Personally, I envision gentle rebukes, constructive criticism, supportive actions, warmness, an absence of judgment, patience, care, and hugs. Think of the people in your life who have been kind to you in contrast to those who have been unkind. What did they do? How did they make you feel? You can define for yourself what self-kindness means to you (but make sure that your definition is helpful to you and doesn't perpetuate or excuse any detrimental and negative habits). Fundamentally, your version of self-kindness should generate feelings of comfort and security. While some negative people may be intolerant toward their flaws, mistakes, or rejection, an individual practicing self-kindness accepts all of those and strives to learn from them. Self-kindness also entails learning coping methods that you can use to support or comfort yourself whenever you feel inadequate, unkind to yourself, or like a failure. Even with self-compassion, you may still fall into negative headspaces from time to time and you may begin to feel negatively about yourself. This isn't a sign that you've regressed, so don't worry. No one can be completely positive all the time! A few rainy days are to be expected and it's normal. The good news is that with self-compassion, you will be better equipped to handle your negative moods and this will prevent a rainy day from turning into a rainy week.

Here is a more detailed guide on defining self-kindness for yourself. You must have a clear idea of what kindness means for you before you can efficiently develop it toward yourself.

Step one: Think about the kindest, most compassionate person that you know. This can be a teacher, family member, friend, mentor, or so on. This person would have been supportive and understanding toward you. If you can't think of anyone you know, try to think of a public figure or even a character from a fictional book or show that you admire for their kindness.

Step two: Reflect and explore what about that person makes you feel like you're cared for or makes you admire them for their kindness. Is it the things they say, their actions, the way they carry themselves?

Step three: Once you have listed down the key factors of your person's kindness, try to use those factors to help you model your self-kindness. Try to provide for yourself what you've realized that your person provides for you. For example, try talking to yourself in the same way that they talk to you, using soothing and loving words. If you feel more cared for through physical touches, such as hugs, repeat this action for yourself. This may seem silly to you but there's a chance it might help you, so try to remain open-minded. You may find that it produces real results and improves your mental state.

Step four: Take a deep breath and check in with yourself. As you receive the feelings of love and kindness from yourself, take mental stock of your emotions and mental state. Learning to be kind to yourself will take a lot of time and effort, but the results are well worth it. So, be patient with yourself and give yourself enough time. Remember that you are just starting to figure out what kindness means to you. Whenever you feel discouraged or impatient with your progress, make time to be grateful to yourself for trying something new.

Mindfulness

Moving on, let's define mindfulness a bit more. Mindfulness is your ability to be present in the moment. It is a psychological state of awareness that allows you to experience what is happening around and inside you without judgment. You must accept your thoughts, emotions, mistakes, and various situations without an intense emotional response. This can prevent you from being too harsh with yourself in difficult times. There are many activities that you may do that may indirectly increase your mindfulness, such as yoga or tai chi; however, mindfulness meditation is the best way for you to actively enhance your ability to be mindful.

Mindfulness meditation focuses your attention and awareness so that you can more easily control your mental processes and thus improve your mental health. If you practice these exercises often, you will obtain a deeper sense of peace, clarity, and concentration. You will also gain cognitive and emotional benefits. On the cognitive side, meditation can increase your concentration, decrease your rumination (where you overthink and have repetitive thoughts about your worries), and improve your working memory. On the emotional side, you will be more accepting and better able to regulate your emotions. Instead of letting your emotions control you, you will be able to control your emotions. In a later chapter, you will be guided through several exercises aimed at increasing your self-compassion, including activities on self-kindness, mindfulness, and common humanity. There will be guidance provided on mindfulness meditation there. For now, let's explore the benefits of mindfulness.

Firstly, as briefly suggested above, mindfulness results in reduced rumination. This is supported by a study done by Richard Chambers et al. (2008) where 20 novice meditators were asked to participate in an intensive mindfulness meditation retreat. This retreat lasted for 10 days and after this time, the group that participated in mindfulness meditation reported significantly higher levels of awareness and lower levels of negative emotions compared to the control group that didn't participate in mindfulness meditation. The mindfulness group also reported feeling fewer depressive symptoms, fewer uncontrollable thoughts, and less time spent ruminating on their anxieties and worries. While everyone is susceptible to worrying, people have different degrees to which they ruminate and obsess over their fears. If you tend to spend hours focusing on what happened in the past or what may happen in the future, then mindfulness would finally allow you to live in the present and take more effective actions from there.

Another benefit of mindfulness is reduced stress. There have been many studies conducted on this topic and the majority of the results are overwhelmingly positive. For example, one experiment conducted by Farb et al. (2010) shows how mindful participants experienced significantly less anxiety and distress compared to the control group of participants who were not mindful. This study involved an eight-week mindfulness-based stress reduction course and results were collected through self-reports on the participants' levels of depression and anxiety. When the neural reactivity of participants was later measured using an fMRI machine after they watched a sad film, the mindfulness group reported fewer negative emotions and had less neural reactivity compared to the control group that didn't go through the mindfulness course. Not only that, the mindfulness group showed different neural responses while watching the sad films than they had displayed before the mindfulness training. This implies that mindfulness improves your emotion regulation strategies so that you're less inclined toward negative emotions and can experience emotions selectively. All in all, this results in reduced levels of stress and distress for you.

Mindfulness can also act as a memory-booster. Most of the time, you may have so much going on in your life simultaneously that key information tends to slip through the cracks. For example, you may forget a friend's birthday, a meeting, or misplace your car keys. Some of these instances of forgetfulness can be explained through proactive interference—when your older memories interfere with your ability to form or access new memories. However, if you regularly participate in mindfulness exercises, you will be able to greatly reduce your proactive interference and thus significantly improve your short-term memory. This can be seen tangibly during a 2005 study done by Lazar et al. which indicated how mindfulness exercises can produce changes in your physical brain. People who go through mindfulness training often experience volume changes in their hippocampus as it increases in size. Your hippocampus is related to your brain's memory functions, so increasing its size greatly optimizes your ability to remember day-to-day information. Other than your short-term memory, mindfulness also improves your working memory and concentration levels. Going back to the study done by Farb et al. in 2010 on novice meditators, the mindfulness group had a better working memory compared to the control group and they were able to sustain their focus for longer periods. Thus, the practice of mindfulness not only improves your short-term memory to benefit you in your everyday life, but it also improves your working memory and concentration levels to benefit you in your professional life.

On the cognitive side, when you practice mindfulness, you are learning to be more aware of your emotions and thoughts by training yourself to not impose judgments or evaluations on them. Some of your cognitive abilities that are involved in being mindful are sustained attention, cognitive flexibility, and cognitive inhibition. Sustained attention refers to your ability to hold your attention at a certain point for a prolonged amount of time. Cognitive flexibility refers to your ability to efficiently shift your thoughts and focus around even when there are distractions in your environment. Cognitive inhibition refers to your ability to suppress certain distracting thoughts that are interfering with your ability to concentrate. All these cognitive abilities are used throughout your day to complete a variety of tasks. By training your mindfulness, you indirectly train these cognitive functions. By doing so, you enable yourself to think more clearly. Your focus will be more intense and more adaptable, allowing you to easily switch from one task to another and allow you to concentrate completely on one task so that you can perform it more efficiently. You will even be able to think faster and adapt to changing information and situations.

Next, mindfulness can lead to stronger relationships. When you are present in the moment, more accepting, and less judgmental, you are more engaged with your friends and family and more attuned to what they're going through. You may notice things you wouldn't have if you were busy battling your negative thoughts and emotions. When you're more accepting, you will be more willing to overlook your partner's flaws or mistakes. Rather than incessantly trying to change your partner, you may become more satisfied with your relationship when you love your partner as they are. This doesn't mean that you don't push them to improve and grow. It does mean that you accept the things that they cannot change and support them to change what they can (at their own pace and if they hold the same values). When you're less judgmental, you will be able to support your loved ones better. Instead of condemning them based on your values, you will be more willing to hear them out, empathize with them, and offer your help.

Common Humanity

Finally, let's learn a little bit more about common humanity or compassion. Compassion literally means "suffering together with another" (Oxford English Dictionary, n.d.) and this suggests how suffering is a mutual and universal experience. So, as a component of self-compassion, common humanity aims to recognize your shared experience of living and learning with others. To do so, you must accept that the human experience is imperfect and sometimes painful. You can't expect to go through your whole life without ever feeling pain or messing up. Suffering and failure are a natural and even useful part of living. It may seem ominous or defeating to think about how life automatically comes with pain and rejection, but when you remember your common humanity, you can remind yourself that these feelings of pain, distress, disappointment, and inadequacy are universal. So, instead of despairing and becoming disconsolate at the idea that there is suffering in the world, you will be able to relate to others and understand that what you're going through is a shared human experience. It's always comforting to know that you're not the only one feeling this way. Simply knowing that others can relate to your situation and empathize with you can be a huge help and a boost to your mood. The situations, triggers, and degree of pain may vary, but the essential point is that everyone can relate to suffering.

One obstacle that you may face in recognizing your common humanity is a false belief or overemphasis on how things 'should' be. For example, when you fail, you may immediately think about how you 'should' be better or how you 'should' have tried harder. Rather than focusing on what you have in common with others, you may narrow your perspective to yourself and become overly preoccupied with thoughts of 'should.' This will lead you to feel embarrassed and worthless, ultimately causing you to disconnect from the world around you and feel isolated. These feelings will cause you to spiral and further prevent you from recognizing your common humanity. Even when things happen to you that aren't in your control, you may focus too much on the 'should' of things and thus not be able to find comfort in your common humanity. For example, if you fall sick, you may worsen your mental state by telling yourself that this shouldn't have happened to you. This type of thinking is highly negative and unproductive. Instead, remember that being sick is part of a common human experience and this may help you accept your situation more readily.

So far, you've explored what self-compassion is and its benefits so you can cultivate self-compassion within yourself. In the next chapter, you will discover the masks of

self-compassion or what self-compassion isn't to strength-
en your practice.

CHAPTER 3

THE MASKS OF SELF- COMPASSION

At the beginning of your journey to self-love, when you are learning self-compassion, there are a few misconceptions that may dissuade you from seriously or effectively practicing it every day. These misconceptions are what you may mistakenly label as self-compassion. Most commonly, people wrongly assume that self-pity, self-indulgence, or self-esteem are the same as self-compassion. From this misunderstanding, you may err in one of two ways. You may either negatively evaluate self-compassion, believing that it is for the weak or morally wrong, unproductive, and indulgent. Or you may begin practicing self-pity, self-indulgence, or negative self-esteem, believing that it is healthy and good since it's technically self-compassion. This is a major mistake as you will be cultivating negative habits that will do serious harm to your mental wellbeing. Even more dangerous is that you may believe that these negative habits are helping you as you're practicing them under the guise of self-compassion.

In this chapter, you will learn how to avoid such harmful misconceptions by studying up on self-pity, self-indulgence, and self-esteem and how they differ from self-compassion. By learning about these masks of self-compassion, you will be able to monitor yourself and differentiate between self-compassion and its masks which will allow you to practice self-compassion safely and effectively.

Firstly, self-compassion is most definitely not self-pity. Self-pity entails being overly focused on your problems, believing that you're the only one facing such terrible problems, and ultimately being immersed in your own negative and self-defeating headspace. When you engage in self-pitying behaviors you may withdraw from others as you forget that they face problems and struggles similar to yours. This is the exact opposite of expressing common humanity which you have learned is an important component of self-compassion.

Other than having you ignore your common humanity and overemphasize the uniqueness of your suffering, self-pity will also lead you to have egocentric feelings about your suffering and uniqueness. Since you falsely believe that your suffering is unique to only you and that others don't suffer as much as you, you may begin to feel entitled to excessive pity, favors, comfort, and attention from others which can be draining and even harmful to friends and family. Self-pity may also cause you to exaggerate the extent of your suffering as you believe that you're suffering more than you actually are. You may become carried away or wrapped up in your emotional and dramatic suffering as you highlight how much you suffer and how the world is against you. People who self-pity may find it difficult to view their situations objectively and rationally. In contrast, self-compassion helps you feel connected with others through your suffering and you're more able to view your situation in the broader human context, allowing for more peace and reason.

Next, self-compassion is also not self-indulgence. When you let yourself get away with everything, when you forgive yourself quickly and without holding yourself accountable for your mistakes, or when you overlook your failures without trying to learn anything from them, you are being self-indulgent rather than self-compassionate. A more specific example would be when you're feeling stressed out about work. A person with self-compassion would acknowledge their feelings and then reflect on why they feel that way and try to resolve those emotions or adjust their work plan for that day to be kinder to themselves. A self-indulgent person would simply choose to forgo all work that day and watch television. If you're still finding it hard to distinguish between these two concepts, it may help to understand self-compassion as a long-term strategy that aims to make you happy and healthy.

Comparatively, self-indulgence is a short-term strategy that aims only to make you happy in the moment, without regard for your future health or happiness. When you're stressed, self-compassion tries to drill down to the cause of that stress to solve it, thus working toward your long-term happiness. Self-compassion also pushes you to keep working, albeit at a kinder and more understanding level. This prevents your work from piling up while still taking your emotions into account. Consequently, you will be less stressed in the future (as you have a bit less work to do). Thus, it's clear that self-compassion takes care of your health and happiness in the long run. Self-indulgence, on the other hand, tells you to forget about work completely and just laze around. Though this may give you temporary pleasure, such actions will harm your well-being in the future as you will become even more stressed about work. The inactivity may even harm your physical health. So, if you mistake self-indulgence for self-compassion and begin practicing it, your long-term health and happiness will decrease.

Alternatively, if you mistake self-indulgence for self-compassion and thus choose to avoid self-compassion, your happiness will also decrease as you may err on the other extreme side of the spectrum. Rather than being too lenient with yourself, you may be too hard on yourself, engaging in destructive criticism or self-flagellation. With such approaches, you will be less productive and less kind to yourself. You will use shame, anger, or hate as motivation and this will be wholly ineffective as your mental state will deteriorate, you will be deathly afraid of failure, and you won't be able to face difficult truths productively. In contrast, self-compassion will act as a strong motivator for you to grow and improve yourself while treating yourself fairly.

Lastly, self-compassion is not self-esteem. Self-esteem can be understood as how much you like yourself and how much you value yourself. This may seem similar to self-compassion but they are distinct concepts. For one, self-esteem often fluctuates with each success or failure while self-compassion is a trait that remains steady throughout your life as long as you practice it and work on it. Self-evaluations do not affect self-compassion, rather self-compassion affects your self-evaluations (by preventing them from being overly critical and helping them to be more realistic and fair).

In tandem with this, since self-esteem is based on your performance and achievements, it also often leads to comparisons. You may base your self-esteem on how well you perform compared to colleagues and peers but with self-compassion, you express your common humanity as you recognize that everyone deserves compassion and understanding and that this isn't reliant on achievements. Instead of comparing yourself with others, you relate yourself to others. All this is not to say that self-esteem is a negative concept. Having healthy self-esteem is a key indicator of good mental health and long-term happiness. The traits of self-esteem mentioned above are not harmful unless they're done out of proportion; however, mistaking self-esteem for self-compassion may still be detrimental as you may try to inflate your self-esteem and this may lead you to bad habits.

Since self-esteem is defined as how much you like yourself or how much you think you're worth, your efforts to raise your self-esteem may lead you to become narcissistic, self-absorbed, or overly critical of others to make yourself look better. You may also become more defensive and explosive whenever someone says or does anything that may make you feel bad about yourself. This will harm your interpersonal relationships. Lastly, trying to boost your self-esteem may make you ignore or distort your unique flaws or failures. This prevents you from seeing yourself clearly and improving yourself. Self-esteem in itself is not a negative construct. You need a high level of self-esteem to increase your happiness and contentment in life; however, mistaking self-esteem for self-compassion has its own dangers, so be careful to protect your self-esteem properly and healthily.

Now that you have a better understanding of the definitions of self-pity, self-indulgence, and self-esteem, and how each of these masks differs from self-compassion, let's learn a bit more about the nuances of each concept.

Self-Pity

There are many expressions of self-pity that may trap you. For example, you may complain incessantly to others about your woes, firmly believing that your experiences of suffering are unique and genuinely feel sorry for yourself. Or you may withdraw from others completely, becoming too wrapped up in your suffering to interact with those around you. Or you may complain incessantly to others about your suffering, but instead of feeling sorry for yourself, you feel no compassion for yourself at all. This particular expression of self-pity is tiring for others and forms a vicious cycle. You pity yourself for going through hard times, but you feel no self-compassion and desire to gain it from others by complaining to them about your troubles. Paradoxically, the more you complain, the more drained or annoyed others may feel, and the less likely they will be to offer you their support. This creates a cycle of unmet needs and a lack of compassion. People who fall into this category of self-pity are usually very hard on themselves and harbor a lot of self-hate. They don't believe that they deserve compassion, but they still crave it which is evident in how they interact with others. Self-compassion would be a way to break the cycle of self-pity as when you have compassion for yourself, you will be less desperate for and reliant on the compassion of others. You will be able to interact with them in a more balanced and reasonable manner. So, as you're practicing self-compassion, it's important to notice whether you're accidentally displaying the self-pitying behaviors described here instead of self-compassion. If so, take some time to realign yourself with self-compassion and, most importantly, keep trying!

The Victim Mentality

Other than being able to recognize self-pitying behaviors, learning about the unique outlook of those experiencing self-pity will also help you to avoid mistaking it for self-compassion. A major trait of self-pity is a victim mentality. People with this mentality often assume that life happens *to* them instead of *for* them. Consequently, they may easily feel personally victimized if something in their life goes awry rather than understanding that something bad is happening around them that they can change or adapt to. Essentially, this mentality is a form of avoidance where the individual chooses not to take any responsibility or accountability for themselves or anything in their life. These people may avoid leaving their comfort zone, being in charge of anything, making hard choices, or doing anything to improve themselves or their situation. Since they believe that things happen *to* them and that they have no control over those things, they allow themselves to be apathetic and passive instead of proactive. This causes them to be stuck where they are and even be controlled by others, all while never living up to their full potential.

There are four clear signs that you have a victim mentality. Firstly, you tend to catastrophize all your problems. This means that you're always assuming the worst. When even a minor inconvenience occurs, you may emphasize it, obsess over it, and make it seem like the end of the world. With this kind of thinking, you create self-fulfilling prophecies where your false assumptions confirm themselves. If you always assume the worst, then you will constantly look for proof that bad things have happened and will continue to happen which confirms your worldview.

The second sign of a victim mentality is a feeling of powerlessness. When you always believe that you're a victim, you necessarily believe that you're being oppressed and that you're powerless to fight against your oppressors. When bad things happen, you assume that the world or the universe is against you. You believe that some vague force is doing this to you, and the vagueness of the perpetrator makes it impossible for you to act against it. When you can break free of your victim mentality, you will realize that no one is making bad things happen to you. Sometimes, bad things just happen. Recognizing this may help you to feel empowered by the fact that you can change your situation.

The third sign that you have a victim mentality is that you engage in negative self-talk. This is because having a victim mentality is closely associated with self-doubt. As previously stated, a victim mentality can be seen as a form of avoidance where the individual doesn't want to be held accountable for themselves. This may spring from a place of self-doubt where they don't believe that they are a capable or competent person. Instead of taking control or trying to improve themselves, they trick themselves into thinking that there's nothing they can do about it anyway. To support this mentality, they may talk down to themselves or be overly critical of themselves. This only reinforces their beliefs and supports their victim mentality. If you have a victim mentality you may also self-sabotage to support your belief of your incapabilities. This will increase your feelings of uselessness and worthlessness, and intensify your negative self-talk.

Lastly, the fourth sign of a victim mentality is that you feel like the world is out to get you. As previously mentioned, you may believe that a vague, undefinable force that you label as the universe or the world is making bad things happen to you. The world may seem like a malevolent force that wants to hurt you and make you miserable.

Breaking Free: Liberating Beliefs, Responsibility, Gratitude, and Positivity

To stop your self-pitying behaviors and your sense of victimhood, you must first accept that you have these traits. Once you accept this, you will be able to shift your thoughts toward self-compassion instead. It will be liberating for you to break out of these negative habits and settle into the healing embrace of self-compassion. The first method of breaking out of self-pity is to identify and challenge your limiting beliefs. Such beliefs are that you're the only person suffering or that you're powerless. While these beliefs may be deeply entrenched in your emotional memory and past experiences, they are detrimental, unproductive, and self-sabotaging. To feel more empowered and compassionate, you must combat and negate these beliefs. Identify your inner voice that supports your feelings of victimhood and self-pity then, challenge that voice with thoughts of taking responsibility, being a survivor, and having the power to change things in your life.

On a related note, another way to break out of self-pity is to take responsibility for your life. Own up to your actions, emotions, and thoughts. Reflect on your values and beliefs, and use these reflections to create the changes that you want in your life. You have the control and power to create and change your reality. When you stop seeing yourself as a victim that life happens to, you will be able to see yourself as an agent of change that influences the world happening around you.

Another way to negate your self-pity is to adopt an attitude of gratitude. When you pity yourself, you may believe that there is never enough of something. For example, you may think that you don't have enough help from others, that you don't have enough advantages in life, that you don't have enough skills to excel, or that you weren't given enough information to do something. In contrast, an attitude of gratitude can make you more aware of the benefits you have in your life. When you practice gratitude, you will be able to appreciate your present reality more. You will stop obsessing over what you don't have and begin to look at the bigger picture and realize what you do have.

Lastly, try to think positively to negate all the negative thoughts that self-pity feeds on. Whenever you're faced with a challenge, rather than pitying yourself or becoming caught up in how alone you are in your suffering, try to find a silver lining and remember that others share in your experience of suffering. Your thoughts have a powerful effect on your reality, so when you start thinking more positively, you will start to feel more positive and your reality will seem more positive.

Self-Indulgence

This is perhaps the most common and efficient mask of self-compassion which deters individuals from practicing it. Since many cultures prohibit being too soft or lenient with yourself, when people assume that self-compassion entails self-indulgence, they become hesitant and negatively judge self-compassion. Rather than being kind to themselves (and being fearful of becoming too lenient with themselves), they revert to the harsh inner critic that they believe will keep them in line and on the right track. This is a common misconception and one that is propagated in many societies, so it bears repeating that being harsh with yourself is not a sustainable or effective way to motivate change for yourself.

To illustrate, imagine a father and a son where the son has just lost a competition. A harsh and critical father may berate the son and say, "You're useless, unskilled, and un-

talented. You'll never be able to win." This may motivate
the son to work harder for a while, but the negative mes-
sages will eventually just depress him and cause him to lose
faith in himself. A compassionate father may say, "I understand that this is disappointing, but losing once doesn't
mean that you'll always lose. Let's figure out what you can
improve on so that you're more prepared next time." This
provides emotional support, encouragement, and a way to
improve moving forward. It acknowledges the son's feelings, improves his confidence, and motivates him to work
harder in the future. It's the same with yourself. Just as you
would expect compassion and comfort from your loved
ones, your mind expects compassion from you. If you're
overly critical of yourself, you will eventually lose motivation; however, with self-compassion, you create long-term
strategies to maintain your motivation and improve. With
this example, I hope you're thoroughly convinced that
being overly critical of yourself is not the proper way to
motivate yourself. Since self-compassion is definitely not
self-indulgence, I also hope that you won't hesitate to begin
practicing self-compassion to increase your self-love.

As for people who are deceived by this mask and mistakenly cultivate habits of self-indulgence rather than
self-compassion there are undeniable consequences. For
one, you don't spend your time productively. Rather, you
indulge too much in short-term pleasures, such as watching television, eating junk food, and sleeping in. These
negative habits lead to countless ramifications such as
weight gain, disconnection from reality, isolation, and so

on. Self-indulgence can cause you to spiral out of control and its negative effects can be dire unless you pull yourself out of it.

Escaping Self-Indulgence: Purpose, Moderation, and Respect

To help you do this, here are some tips on moving away from self-indulgence and moving toward self-compassion. Firstly, stick to your purpose. Whenever you want to exhibit self-indulgent behaviors, try to reflect and discover what objective you're trying to avoid or what larger, general goals you have in your life. Practicing self-compassion over self-indulgence would mean that you keep pursuing those goals. Whether your actions that day work toward your goal quickly or not, the point is to keep taking positive action. The contentment you gain from that will be much more satisfying than any temporary pleasure you gain from self-indulgence. If it's not feasible for you to take action toward your goals for that day, don't use that as a pass to over-indulge. Rather, you can do something altruistic which aligns with your values, such as volunteering or helping a friend. Being able to contribute to the world while affirming your morals and ethics will create long-term happiness compared to the short-term pleasures of self-indulgence.

Another critical strategy to combat self-indulgence is to practice self-restraint. Even when you realize the difference between self-compassion and self-indulgence, it may be difficult for you to choose the former over the latter since self-indulgence promises immediate pleasure. This is where self-restraint comes in. You must make a conscious effort to balance responsible and pleasurable activities. This is a lifelong practice but avoiding the negative habits of self-indulgence sets the groundwork for you to cultivate the positive habits of self-compassion.

Finally, you must treat yourself with love and respect. Someone who binge eats two tubs of ice cream or someone who lazes in bed for hours on end isn't treating themselves with love or respect. You must take care of your needs and supply yourself with all that you need to flourish and be happy. The habits of self-indulgence don't do this but the habits of self-compassion do. Whenever you're tempted to be self-indulgent, remind yourself that you need to respect your body and mind, and be loving toward yourself.

Self-Esteem

As you've read, self-esteem refers to how much you like yourself and your sense of personal value or worth. Self-esteem is often lowest during childhood when you are still getting to know yourself. Then, in adulthood, your self-esteem grows as your personality and outlook on life solidify. Throughout your life, however, your self-esteem changes. Many factors continually act upon your self-esteem which we will explore soon, but for now, let's discuss the individual components of your self-esteem.

Confidence

The first component is confidence. This relates to your belief and assurance in your abilities, competence, and self-efficacy. This component relates to competence which you will learn about later. When your feelings of competence rise, your feelings of confidence will rise as well. If you have good confidence, you will be more willing to face new challenges and situations, believing that you can achieve most things if given enough time, effort, and practice. Whether you succeed or fail, your confidence will allow you to persevere and keep pursuing your goals.

Security

A feeling of security will also help increase your confidence. When you feel secure in your environment and your relationships are stable, you will feel more confident in your ability to face challenges. Having security in your life and your relationships means that you will have the mental capacity to access external support and social networks. These, in turn, will help you feel safe, accepted, cared for, and stable. All this is important in developing your confidence and peace of mind.

Identity

Your sense of identity is also vital for your self-esteem. Knowing yourself and having a stable sense of self will help you interact with others and the world in a way that aligns with your values. Your identity will rarely be just one thing. You will usually assign yourself various labels to help you make sense of how you relate to a variety of situations and in different relationships. Your sense of identity must be flexible and multi-faceted or else you risk losing your sense of self if a pillar of your identity (a job, family role, etc.) changes. This is a normal and healthy way to conceive of your identity. People with unhealthy levels of self-esteem may be overly fixated on one part of their identity, making their sense of identity rigid and one-dimensional. With their entire sense of self riding on one version of themselves, they may be prone to feeling empty, anxious, or lacking a coherent self. To avoid this, you need to consciously invest your sense of self in diverse interests, relationships, and contexts.

Purpose

Self-esteem also relates to your sense of purpose. If you have no direction in your life, you will have no goals, no sense of achievement, and no way to find long-term happiness. If you choose for yourself what your aims are and work toward them, you will have healthier self-esteem as you are living life according to your values and desires. When you achieve your goals, you will feel happy and accomplished, and when you work toward your higher purpose, you will feel content and fulfilled.

Competence

The last component of self-esteem is your feelings of competence. When you allow yourself to leave your comfort zone and confront difficult and daunting challenges, you may increase your feelings of competence as you either overcome those challenges or survive them. Even if you fail, you will be more confident in your ability to face new things. Feelings of competence also stem from your past achievements, your current assessment of your skills and abilities, and the evaluations of others. All these elements can tangibly show you your level of competence. When you believe that you're competent, your self-esteem will rise. Your trust in yourself will also rise, as will the trust that others place in you. Affirming to yourself that you're trustworthy and capable of being independent will greatly raise your self-esteem. You will also be able to feel a sense of contribution as you will be more willing to help out others according to your ability. This will increase your feeling of influence as your competence enables you to make a difference in the lives of others by helping them.

Now that you understand the components of self-esteem, let's explore the factors that affect self-esteem throughout your life.

- Age: As you've read, age plays a role in self-esteem. As you age, you gain more competence and solidify your sense of self, thus your self-esteem tends to increase as you get older.

- Racism and discrimination: If you've experienced racism or discrimination, your self-esteem may be lower as others have negatively assessed you based on something you have no control over.

- Genetics: Your genes may affect your self-esteem as they code for certain personality traits that may affect your competence in certain areas and how you interact with yourself and the world.

- Relationships: If you have healthy, supportive relationships, your self-esteem will be nourished. If you have unhealthy, critical, toxic relationships, your self-esteem will suffer.

- Worker identity: If you identify as a worker, your self-esteem may increase. This may be because you feel more competent, trusted, and able to make a difference in your life and the lives of others.

- Education: Having higher education may lead to higher self-esteem as you feel more accomplished and you're able to obtain a higher income.

- Living alone: If you live alone, you may be more prone to feelings of isolation and overly critical thoughts. This may lead to low self-esteem.

- Disability: If you have a physical or mental disability, you may have less confidence in your competence and thus have lower self-esteem.

- Body image: Many people's self-esteem is affected by how they and others view their physical bodies based on the beauty standards of their society.

Since countless factors in your life affect your self-esteem, it's important to maintain it at a healthy level by honestly checking in with yourself. At the beginning of this chapter, you were told of the dangers of mistaking self-esteem for self-compassion; however, I want to reiterate that self-esteem is not a negative concept. In fact, it is highly important in your life. It's just that there are healthy levels of self-esteem and unhealthy levels of self-esteem. Just like there are healthy ways to increase your self-esteem and unhealthy ways to do so. It's highly recommended that you take care of your self-esteem in healthy ways. Your self-esteem is important as it impacts your decision-making process. If you have healthy self-esteem, you will have a positive, realistic view of your potential and abilities, and this may increase your motivation and inspiration to face new challenges. If you have low self-esteem, you may doubt yourself too much and be less motivated to try your best or try new things. With overly high self-esteem, you may overestimate your skills and take on too much.

Your level of self-esteem also influences your relationships. With a healthy amount of self-esteem, you will have a happy, realistic, rational relationship with yourself and this will enable you to have such relationships with others. People with low self-esteem may have trouble accepting affection from others and expressing their needs in relationships. People with overly high self-esteem may criticize others too much, view themselves as perfect, and block themselves from self-improvement.

Your self-esteem is also deeply connected to your emotional health. With healthy self-esteem, you will be able to understand your needs and provide them for yourself. You will also be confident and realistic with yourself. With low self-esteem, you may feel unworthy of love and incapable. Whereas with overly high self-esteem, you may be deluding yourself as to your abilities and damage your relationships by being overly critical.

With your self-esteem affecting so many aspects of your life, you need to develop healthy self-esteem. But how can you tell if you have healthy, low, or overly high self-esteem? To answer these questions, I have provided the signs of healthy self-esteem below.

- You don't dwell on negative experiences from your past.
- You don't think you're better or worse than others. You see yourself as an equal.
- You're able to express your needs and desires.
- You have justified confidence in your abilities.
- You have a positive outlook on life.
- You're able to be assertive and say no.

- You have a realistic view of your strengths and weaknesses, and you can accept them.

- You appreciate yourself and those around you.

- You enjoy improving yourself and finding meaning in your life.

- You have loving, supportive, and respectful relationships.

- You know what your values are and live your life by those values.

- You can calmly and kindly share your opinions with others and you can accept when they don't agree with you.

Having healthy self-esteem is monumentally beneficial for you as you will be able to motivate yourself more efficiently, feel more capable, have healthy boundaries, and maintain healthy relationships.

Having low self-esteem may express itself in your life in a variety of ways. You may have low self-esteem if you identify with the statements below.

- You believe that others are better than you.

- You find it difficult to express your needs and desires.

- You tend to focus on your weaknesses and ignore your strengths.

- You frequently doubt yourself or feel fearful and anxious.

- You have a negative view of life and feel like you're not in control.

- You have an intense fear of failure.

- You find it hard to accept compliments or positive feedback.

- You can't say no or set healthy boundaries for yourself.

- You put others' needs before your own all the time.

- You find it hard to pursue your aims and maintain healthy relationships.

Having low self-esteem may lead to several unhealthy habits and thoughts, and you may even develop a mental illness such as anxiety or depression. Even if you don't develop these conditions, having low self-esteem will invariably produce negative impacts on your life and thus lower your general quality of life. On the other hand, when you have excessive self-esteem, you may exhibit the following traits, so read carefully and reflect upon them.

- You obsess over being perfect.
- You believe you're always right.
- You think that you can't fail.

- You compare yourself with others often and conclude that you're better or more skilled than everyone.

- You have grandiose ideas.

- You tend to overestimate your abilities and skills.

- You are defensive and don't respond well to criticism.

- You experience difficulties in relationships and social situations.

Having excessive self-esteem (or, in other terms, being narcissistic) is dangerous to yourself and others. People who exhibit the traits of excessive self-esteem such as those listed above are prone to high levels of aggression. This can manifest itself in the form of physical threats, verbal abuse, spreading gossip, bullying people, or exploding and releasing aggression on innocent bystanders.

Narcissism

Narcissists may often exhibit behavior that is threatening or intend to harm others. Some may do so in a heated, explosive manner while others may do so in a cool, penetrating manner. Either way, people with excessive self-esteem, which ironically they have a lack of self-esteem (you can find more answers to this topic in my book A Woman's Confidence Code), tend to be more aggressive than those with healthy or low self-esteem. One reason may be because they feel superior to others and have an exceptionally low perception of others, so it's no big deal to them if they attack and harm others. They may even think that others deserve this abuse due to their inferiority. Such a mindset will directly harm those around you and indirectly harm your quality of life as you will be deluded and unloved. Other dangers of excessive self-esteem have to do with your personality. Narcissists are usually prejudiced, discriminate, lack empathy, and are bad partners. Since they see themselves as superior, they will easily hold negative biases against strangers and even their loved ones. This can skew their perceptions and prevent them from being grounded in reality. Narcissists will also be low in empathy as they don't think others deserve their compassion. Empathy is the ability to imagine what others are going through and it requires a firm grip on reality. Excessive self-esteem, often based on delusions that are far from reality, can make this difficult. Narcissists will even be bad partners as they may be self-centered, stubborn, judgmental, unreasonable, disrespectful, and demanding. Overall, having excessive self-esteem is dangerous to those around you and is also harmful to yourself, so it is important to stay vigilant and reflect often lest you find yourself described as uncompassionate, unempathetic, unloving, unreasonable, and removed from reality.

Excessive self-esteem can often be mistaken for confidence or healthy self-esteem but the key difference is that excessive self-esteem tends to be more unstable, shifting according to your current situation. If you have healthy self-esteem, you will be more able to handle any factors that may hurt your self-perception. You can ensure you have healthy self-esteem rather than low or excessive self-esteem through self-compassion. Practicing self-compassion often is a sign of having healthy self-esteem as you provide yourself with a stable sense of self-worth. In a later chapter, you will learn about how you can increase your self-compassion. For now, let's briefly look at how you can improve your self-esteem.

Improving Self-Esteem

Firstly, become aware of your negative and critical thoughts. Once you can identify your distorted thoughts that decrease your self-esteem, you will be able to challenge them. Try countering these negative thoughts with positive ones or ones that consider reality more.

Concerning this, try to use more positive self-talk. For example, recite positive affirmations to yourself. Some useful affirmations that you can repeat to yourself are listed below. For maximum benefits, try to recite them while looking in the mirror.

- My mistakes are not final. They're simply a stepping stone to success and a bump along the path that I am forging to achieve my dreams.
- I will continue to improve myself, learn, and grow.
- I am deserving of happiness, success, and a good life.

- I don't need to suffer or be miserable.

- I am competent, smart, and capable.

- I am growing myself and changing for the better.

- I love the person that I am becoming.

- I trust in my skills and abilities.

- I have good ideas.

- I make helpful contributions.

- I have intrinsic worth.

To make these affirmations more effective, remember to use the present tense. This will affirm your value in the moment and it won't make your worth contingent on a point in the future. Your affirmations should also be positively worded. For example, instead of saying "I'm not worthless" you should say, "I have worth." This is a more powerful statement. Finally, your affirmations should make you feel good about yourself in a realistic and relevant manner.

Some other strategies that can increase your self-esteem are spending time with people who are supportive and encouraging, helping others, and making time to celebrate your achievements. When implementing these strategies, change what you can and accept what you can't. In other words, don't chase perfection and take it one day at a time. In this chapter, you've learned about the three masks of self-compassion (self-pity, self-indulgence, and self-esteem) so that you don't get trapped by any of them as you strive for self-compassion. In the next chapter, you will learn about the first step in the LOVE system: embracing your inner critic.

CHAPTER 4

SELF-CRITICISM VS SELF-REFLECTION

The first step in the LOVE system is to embrace your inner critic. To do so, we must first understand the difference between self-criticism (destructive and constructive) and self-reflection. In Chapter 1 you discovered the differences between destructive criticism and constructive criticism. From there, you realized that criticism in itself is not harmful. In fact, criticism is needed for you to live a happy and fulfilling life.

You need criticism to open your eyes to harmful behaviors that are preventing you from reaching your goals or fulfilling your potential. Destructive criticism can indeed lead to self-deprecating behavior but criticism done properly can be transformative. By being open to criticism, you enhance the quality of your work, actions, thoughts, and self-awareness. Being able to evaluate every part of your life will help you to weed out the bad and nurture the good. If you never criticize yourself, you will never know what was good or bad, where you could have improved, why a certain outcome came to be, or how you could have learned from your experiences. Being self-critical also helps you to avoid repeating your mistakes. When you criticize yourself for certain actions, you become more aware of those habits and more able to act against them. This will prevent you from making the same errors in the future.

Your self-criticism may often take a turn for the worse and become destructive. In times like this, a solution and a positive alternative to destructive criticism is self-reflection. Through self-reflection, you can develop resilience against destructive criticism. When your destructive criticism rears its head and you begin to feel doubtful, fearful, anxious, worthless, and sad, self-reflection can calm your body and mind by understanding how your destructive criticism isn't based on solid logic nor is it helpful or productive.

Through self-reflection, you will be able to recognize that your criticism affects your motivation and wellbeing. You will thus be more inclined to use constructive criticism and self-compassion to motivate yourself. Your self-reflection will also make you more accepting and realistic with yourself. This will negate your destructive criticism which is usually based on unrealistic expectations and unkind assumptions about yourself. Self-reflection allows you to acknowledge your abilities and view your skills in a realistic light. Though destructive criticism does affect your physical brain, it's important to remember that your brain has neuroplasticity and can continue changing and altering, so it's never too late to change your habits and rewire how your brain works. Instead of destructive criticism, begin to train yourself in self-reflection. To do this, let's explore the differences between these two concepts.

Differences Between Destructive Self-Criticism and Productive Self-Reflection

As you know, destructive self-criticism is the inner voice that automatically speaks up in a demeaning and devaluing manner whenever you're faced with rejection, uncertainty, failure, or negative feedback. Such inner dialogue is unhelpful, demotivating, and limiting. In contrast, self-reflection is defined as meditation or serious, concentrated thought about your character, actions, and motives. It occurs when you take a step back and objectively reflect on your life, beliefs, assumptions, and habits. Everyone has the capacity for self-reflection. This capacity allows you to connect with yourself in a more realistic and considerate manner, realize the negative habits you have, maintain your motivation to reach your goals, look at the bigger picture, soothe and support yourself through negative emotions, identify your goals and values, and increase your insight and wisdom. When you self-reflect, you will discover information about what went wrong and what you can do differently next time to increase your chances of success. This skill can then be applied when thinking of constructive criticism to confront a specific challenge in your personal or professional life. Without self-reflection, there can be no constructive criticism.

Unlike destructive criticism which blames your character and personality for your failures, self-reflection focuses on changeable behaviors and mindsets. While destructive criticism is subjective and harsh, self-reflection is objective and assumes a wider, general view to discover what you can improve on.

Another difference between these two concepts is the time and energy you put into them. With destructive criticism, you typically spend a lot of time lost in ruminations without putting energy into it. Your negative thoughts will keep coming up whether you want them to or not, but with self-reflection, you must exert a lot of energy to reflect for prolonged periods. It's not an easy feat to objectively assess and reflect on your behavior. You must think long and hard to have a productive session of reflection.

Another notable difference between these two concepts is the effect they have on your performance. Destructive criticism may encourage you to work harder for the moment, but eventually, it will harm your confidence and hinder your performance. Meanwhile, self-reflection will give you a more realistic view of your skills and abilities, and this will increase your confidence. Self-reflection will also give you feasible and productive ways to improve yourself, which will lead to better performance.

Benefits of Self-Reflection

Now that you understand the differences between self-reflection and destructive self-criticism, let's explore the importance of self-reflection. As mentioned previously, self-reflection demands a lot of time and energy from you. This is why many people choose not to practice it. If you don't cultivate self-reflection, you will be missing out on countless benefits.

Awareness

Firstly, self-reflection leads to a greater amount of self-awareness. Being self-aware will help you understand yourself at a deeper level and this will help you be more at peace with yourself and live with intention. You will know what ideals you have and consciously work toward them. This will then increase your confidence and self-esteem. Additionally, self-reflection provides you with an objective perspective on how you live your life. When you step back and take in your whole situation, you may gain a new understanding as you are no longer limited by your narrow outlook. Being able to concentrate on the big picture will prevent you from being too focused on small setbacks and

issues. You will even become more open-minded and accepting of new perspectives.

Conscious Decision-Making

The next benefit of self-reflection is that it allows you to
respond to sudden change instead of reacting instinctively.
In the heat of the moment, you don't often think about the
consequences of your words and actions and may jump to
conclusions when you don't consider the context of your
situation. Impulsive decisions made under emotional distress may end up being those that regret later on. When you
take time to self-reflect, you will behave more thoughtfully
and carefully, adapting to new challenges rather than esca-
lating the conflict. Once you have a better understanding
of your thoughts and emotions, you will be more useful in
a time of crisis and be able to approach any situation in a
more calm and collected way.

Deeper Understanding

Other than that, self-reflection can help you retain new
knowledge and skills. Self-reflection is a critical part of
learning as, no matter what you've learned (be it an aca-
demic subject or life experience), reflecting on it will give
you time to digest, consider, and integrate the information
into your life. You will retain the information better with
this deeper understanding and be able to apply it in your
day-to-day life.

Confidence

Through self-reflection, you can understand what's working for you and what's not. From there, you can take positive actions to work on your weaknesses, and focus on your strengths. Each time you improve, you will gain more confidence and increase your self-knowledge. This will then lead you to make better decisions about your abilities.

Challenging Prejudice

Finally, self-reflection can help you to challenge your assumptions. As you grow up, you may have collected many biases and assumptions that you believe to be true; however, if you never challenge them, you will never weed out the prejudiced, or hurtful assumptions that you have. An obvious type of assumption that you should challenge is your limiting beliefs. Sometimes, such beliefs are true and meant to protect you. Other times, they're false and based on fear and doubt. Take a step back and debate with yourself about the validity of such beliefs and whether they align with your values and how you wish to treat others. This will help you reflect on what beliefs are false and hinder you from reaching your full potential and connecting with others

Just as there are benefits for when you self-reflect, there are consequences for when you don't. When you don't practice self-reflection, you may stay in a position or situation that's not conducive or friendly to yourself. You may stay in an abusive relationship, you may stay in a job that is too easy for you, or you may stay in a situation that causes you anxiety or stress. Eventually, you may tire yourself out and crash and burn. Rather than mindlessly moving forward in a situation that's not good for you, take the time to stop, remove yourself from the situation for a while, and give yourself time to reflect. This will help you realize what's important for you and hopefully persuade you to take some positive actions.

Switching From Self-Criticism to Self-Reflection

So far, you've learned about how self-reflection differs from self-criticism and how self-reflection benefits you. Knowing the theories behind these concepts will help you choose to stop being destructively critical of yourself and start practicing self-reflection; however, wanting to self-reflect and knowing how to do so effectively are two different things. It can be hard to know where to start to achieve such a momentous goal, so here is a detailed guide to self-reflection in four steps.

- Stop: Take a step back from your situation by physically or mentally removing yourself from the conflict.

- Look: Try to gain an objective perspective on what is happening.

- Listen: Be still and quiet as you search for your inner guide and the wisdom to speak up. Give yourself ample time and space for this step.

- Act: Identify what steps you need to take to move forward, improve, and adapt. The key here is measurable progress and tangible results rather than an intention alone.

As you perform these steps, remember that you only need to reflect on: yourself and the areas of your life that are important to you. The actions of others and their feelings are outside of your control. While reflecting on yourself, think about who you are and your goals. Create an inventory of your core values and beliefs, guiding principles, priorities, unique skills, passions, strengths, and any weaknesses you must be aware of. Then, think outside of yourself about what impact you want to make on others, how you want to add value to the world, what your passions are, and what limiting assumptions you were raised with. When reflecting on the areas of your life that are important to you, try to consider multiple spheres such as your relationships, family, career, spirituality, and health. As you consider each sphere of your life, write them in order of importance and rate your performance in each of those areas on a scale of one to 10. This will help you see where you excel and which area needs more attention.

Some more detailed questions to ask yourself while you're self-reflecting are:

- How do you feel about a certain area of your life?

- How would you rate your success or satisfaction in a certain area on a scale of 1– 10?

- What's helping you succeed in life? What's contributing to your failures?

- What do you want more or less of?

- What are your accomplishments?

- What are your hopes and goals?

- What are you grateful for?

- How do you want to improve a specific area of your life?

Other than knowing what questions to ask, it's helpful to know when to self-reflect. Hopefully, you plan to make self-reflection a part of your daily routine until it becomes a habit as this will produce more benefits for you. You can choose to reflect every month or every week. The more often you reflect, the sooner new insights will be revealed. Adjust your reflection sessions according to how busy you are so you don't tire yourself out by exerting time and energy that you do not have. It may seem tiring to reflect daily but it's the best way for you to make it a habit. Many prefer to reflect in the morning or at night when it is quiet.

Some people feel especially motivated to self-reflect on special occasions such as a birthday, the start of a new year, or an anniversary. When celebrating a new year, you can evaluate the past year and compare your intentions and goals with what you were able to achieve. You can also consider new goals and desires for the year ahead. When you reach milestones (such as birthdays, anniversaries, or religious events), you can reflect on how you want to change or improve going forward.

Then there are occasions that require self-reflection. For example, after a bad performance review or a fight with your friend, you must take some time to self-reflect on what went wrong. As soon as you accept that you're on the wrong track, step back and think about what happened. This will help you avoid similar events in the future. You will know that you're off track because you will be unhappy, demotivated, and stressed.

Journaling and Meditation

For a greater chance of success, consider writing down your thought process in a dedicated notebook. Doing so may help you to reach deeper levels of understanding, remember your thoughts, return to certain thoughts later, and reduce your levels of anxiety. Many find it beneficial to journal in bed at the end of the day to relax and let go of the day's stress while others prefer to journal in the morning and start their day with purpose. Plus, once the thought or goal is on the page in front of you, you will be able to more readily let it go or confront it.

Consider carrying a small notepad or a phone with you so that you can write down any fleeting epiphanies to consider later. My biggest self-reflection trigger is when I feel a conflict of values within myself. When my response to a situation doesn't agree with my values, I write down exactly what happened and take a step back as soon as possible to consider the value in conflict, as well as the situation. Next, I schedule a time to self-reflect and hold myself accountable for those plans. You can do this by creating a reminder in your calendar or by telling your partner or friend about your plans so that they can hold you accountable. If you have someone to report back to, you will feel more compelled to do the work.

Moreover, try to be a neutral observer when you're reflecting on conflict, especially when intense emotions are involved. If you write as if you were a fly on the wall, you will notice the difference between what actually happened and how you interpreted the situation to receive greater insights into your behavior.

Finally, try meditation. There are countless benefits to meditation and one of them is that it can allow your inner wisdom to break through. When you quiet your mind, your higher self will speak to you and provide clarity. You will learn more about meditation techniques in a later chapter.

The ultimate goal of this book is fostering self-love through the LOVE system and thus far, we have taken the first step by learning about self-compassion and how to achieve it through self-reflection and embracing your inner critic.

The next chapters will explain the LOVE system letter by letter, building on the skills you have learned so far with targeted exercises and examples. The second step is "L" where you lure the voice in your head toward compassion. Don't worry, you will receive many exercises to help you do this. So, without any further delay, let's start on step two!

CHAPTER 5

LURE THE VOICE IN YOUR HEAD WITH COMPASSION

So far, you've gained a lot of theoretical knowledge to help you make the right decisions and to prevent you from inadvertently causing more harm than good in your journey of self-improvement. All that knowledge will serve as a map that can show you the way to self-love. Over the next four steps of the LOVE system, you will receive practical knowledge to pair with your theoretical knowledge. If theoretical knowledge is the map that will guide you, then practical knowledge is the tool that will increase your chances for success and make you more efficient.

In this chapter, you will supplement all that you have just learned about switching from destructive self-criticism to constructive self-reflection by learning how to be compassionate toward yourself. This will make it easier for you to switch from negative self-talk to positive self-reflection by luring your inner critic toward a more compassionate approach. While this may seem daunting, you will be led through various simple but effective exercises to discover how to interact with your unique inner critic.

The Friend Approach

The first way to foster self-compassion is by treating yourself as you would treat a good friend that you love and care for. Think about if this applies to you: When your friend messes up or fails, do you find it easy to offer them love, support, understanding, and compassion? But when you make the same mistake or face the same failure, do you beat yourself up without applying the same support and compassion to yourself? This perspective-taking exercise aims to have you treat yourself with the same love and compassion that you would treat your friends with. It can be done in four simple steps!

Step one: Think about the times when your close friend felt bad about themself or was struggling. How did you respond to them and treat them? Write down what you did, what you said, what tone you used, and so on in as much detail as possible.

Step two: Think about the times when you felt bad about yourself or were struggling. How did you respond and treat yourself? Write down what you did or what you typically do in such situations.

Step three: Compare what you wrote in the first two steps. Is there a difference? Why is there a difference? Ask yourself why you may treat yourself so differently and what fears or beliefs influence that.

Step four: Write down how you think things may change if you treated yourself like you would treat your friends.

The Self-Compassion Break

The second exercise you can try to increase your self-love and self-awareness is called the self-compassion break. This exercise can be done in three steps:

Step one: Recall a situation in your life that is causing you stress or pain (or recall a past event that caused you similar emotions).

Step two: Allow yourself to reflect and think about this situation. Take extra notice of how you feel as you bring the memory forward. How did or does it make you feel, emotionally and physically? Get in touch with your body's response and identify the emotions it elicits in you.

Step three: Recite helpful and affirming statements to yourself while acknowledging your distress. For example, accept that this is a moment of suffering, recognize that you're feeling stressed or sad, and admit that suffering is a part of life. These affirmations will activate your mindfulness and help you realize your common humanity. You will be able to verbalize what you're feeling toward the situation (thus helping you understand yourself more) and tell yourself that this suffering is unavoidable and that other human beings share in this experience of suffering.

As an extension of this third step, you can physically comfort yourself by hugging yourself, squeezing your hands together, placing your hands gently over your heart, or holding a comfort item. You can also continue to recite soothing statements such as that other people also feel like this sometimes, that you're not alone, that everyone struggles, or that you can and should be kind to yourself. You can even use specific phrases that are more relevant to your current situation and ask yourself for patience or forgiveness. This short exercise should bring great relief and prove that you can acknowledge and accept your suffering while taking care of yourself by being kind, patient, and loving to yourself.

Letter Writing

The third exercise to increase your self-compassion involves writing a letter and consists of three parts. I call the
first part, "Naming Your Thoughts and Emotions." To begin this part, think about the imperfections, flaws, and failures that make you feel bad about yourself. What don't you
like about yourself? What makes you feel like you're not
good enough? What are you insecure about? Your answers
can be general or specific to a particular issue you're facing
at the moment. Then, notice how you feel when you think
about these things. Name each emotion and let yourself
experience them in turn. When confronting your negative
feelings (which are a natural result of listing your insecuri-
ties) and allowing yourself to feel them, you are practicing
mindfulness by letting the discomfort come and go while
being less judgmental. You will come to believe that our
negative emotions aren't inherently harmful or bad. Rather, they're a natural part of life, they can provide you with
more self-knowledge, and they can even provoke positive
results such as self-compassion. As you feel all your emotions, write about them.

Once you've done this, you can move on to the second
part: "A Letter From a Friend." In this part, you write a
letter to yourself from the perspective of a loving friend.
This is similar to the first exercise you learned (the friend
approach). You will imagine how you would treat a friend
and apply those thoughts, actions, and words to yourself.
Imagine how a loving friend would write to you as they see

you, accept you, support you, and understand you. Imagine that this friend knows everything about you and the choices, contexts, and circumstances that made you. In the letter, try to emulate the qualities of a loving friend while still focusing on the flaws and imperfections that you wrote about in part one. How would they approach the issue? Would they understand and support you? Would they hold you to impossible standards and judge you?

Part three is called "Reading the Letter." Put the letter you've written down and walk away for a few moments. Don't immediately read what you've written. Give yourself some time and space to breathe and then come back and read it. As you do this, try to let the words really sink in. Understand the meaning of what you've written and try to absorb and accept it. Don't read this letter as a note you just wrote but pretend that you have just received it from an unconditionally loving friend. Open your heart up to the compassion in the letter. Allow yourself to feel it and be soothed and comforted. Try to turn the writer's compassion into compassion for yourself.

Confront Your Critic

This exercise aims to redirect your overly self-critical inner voice to produce positive change through conversation. Instead of becoming another harsh critic, you will take on a constructive and compassionate guiding voice when addressing your inner voice as a separate entity. This is an exercise that you can keep doing throughout your life as you will always need to protect yourself against habits of destructive criticism.

Step one: Notice your inner critic. Pay careful attention when you're being critical of yourself and notice the words, statements, tone, and assumptions that you use. Often you may not notice when you're being overly self-critical but a sudden low mood may be an indicator. This first step will already require a lot of practice but you will gradually get better at noticing how you talk to yourself. This will train your self-awareness as you start to notice more and more how you treat yourself negatively and how this may be affecting you. If you start to feel frustrated, remember that forcing yourself to confront the reality of how you view and treat yourself is not easy. Although this step may bring up intensely negative emotions, the next two steps will help you feel more positive.

Step two: Argue with your critic. Begin to combat and challenge the self-criticism you noticed in step one. Whenever you notice yourself starting to talk negatively toward yourself, talk back to that voice to try to negate it. Be careful not to adopt the same critical or harsh tone that it uses as this will only heighten your self-judgment rather than lower it. Instead, use compassion and facts to debate and challenge your critical inner voice. You can first validate how nervous, sad, angry, worried, or afraid it feels, but also tell it that it's causing you a lot of unnecessary distress. Tell the voice that, despite its best intentions, it's not helping you and that you would like it to try using compassion instead.

   Step three: Change your inner dialogue. Now you can gradually rework the assumptions and observations made by your inner critic. Instead of approaching this negotiation with a negative and defeatist attitude, try to see it from the eyes of a compassionate friend with whom you're trying to compromise. This may help you be more supportive and positive. Try to reason with this voice and be patient if it resists the change at first but be firm with what changes you need.

Personal Inventory

The fifth exercise involves identifying what you really want and motivating you to achieve everything in healthy and effective ways. The first step of this exercise is called "Taking Stock" and it involves the steps of the previous exercise. You must think about what you excessively criticize yourself for while also recognizing the emotional pain that this criticism causes you and opening yourself up to self-compassion. This step aims to eradicate the harm done to your motivation by your negative self-talk. As you're noticing and challenging your overly harsh inner critic, try to investigate what it's trying to push you toward. Sometimes your destructive criticism is wholly irrational and unrealistic, but other times it's based on a deeper goal or desire you have. If you can't figure out any goals or aims from your inner critic, simply reflect on yourself and ask yourself what your deeper aims and aspirations are. This will train your self-reflection and if you need more help and guidance for this step, you can always refer back to "Switching from Self-Criticism to Self-Reflection" in Chapter 4.

Step two is called "New Ways." Once you've challenged your negative self-talk and figured out your goals in life, push yourself to create new, kinder, more caring ways to motivate yourself. Imagine how your loved ones may go about motivating you.

Step three is called "Routine Checks." Sustain your new motivational habits by repeating step one whenever you catch yourself being overly self-critical or negative; however, don't try to overcome your negative inner voice by pushing it away. Instead, allow yourself to feel the negative emotions that your critical voice brings, accept your emotions, then offer yourself compassion. After opening yourself up to compassion, try to reframe your perspectives and beliefs (repeating step two).

My Experience

This exercise was especially helpful for me as I used to feel absolutely awful without realizing why. I would beat myself up emotionally, attacking every part of myself and my life. I felt like I was doing everything wrong, but the vagueness of this self-sabotaging prevented me from doing anything helpful about my emotions. One late fall morning, I woke up to a head full of chaos and negative voices. I just couldn't pull myself together. My husband was off at work, so I put my four-year-old on the bus to preschool, checked that my two-year-old was happily playing with my live-in nanny, and went upstairs to be alone. I wanted to close myself off from the world and reflect on my thoughts and emotions. The second I stopped and allowed myself to feel everything that I was feeling, I was overwhelmed with guilt. My mind was hijacked by a whirlwind composed of my negative voice and everyone else's comments (real and imagined) about how I was letting people down. I tried to calm myself and did the exercise described above. I had already been doing it for a while to try to figure out what all my self-criticism was trying to achieve. That day, thankfully, I realized what I really wanted out of life.

That same morning, I quit my job as a financial advisor at a financial firm in New York. This job was not just a job—it was a representation of my earlier dreams and ambitions. Quitting didn't just mean leaving the job—it meant giving up on my dreams, my parent's faith in me, and their efforts in educating me. This was not an easy decision, but the more I reflected on my emotions and what I wanted in life, the more I realized that the fulfillment I got from parenting my children was bigger than my desire for a career.

Of course, I value having a career and I think every woman should pursue their ambitions if they want to. Through my reflections, however, I realized that the toll my professional life was taking on my family life was making me overly critical of myself. It was taking 12 hours a day out of my life with evening follow-ups and I was often drained and depleted when spending time with my family. I felt like I was missing precious time with them and my marriage was suffering. Although I had every right to pursue my ambitions and career goals, I could not spread my time out the way I wanted to. After some reflection, I realized that I wanted and needed to focus more on my family regardless of everyone's expectations or the judgments of others. Quitting that type of a job and exploring other options was the right decision for me but I would be lying if I said it was not a painful one.

Before trying this exercise, I could not communicate my needs to anyone as I didn't know what my needs were. I could not address my destructive criticism as it was too vague (I didn't realize that all my guilt was coming from my lackluster family life). I felt disconnected from my life and unbalanced. I was so focused on meeting everyone else's needs (my husband's and kids' needs, my parents' needs, my company's needs) that I didn't stop to think about what I wanted or needed. Through this exercise, I hope you will arrive at your own realizations and "Aha" moments.

Many other women may fall into this same trap. You may think that caring for others means caring for yourself, but this isn't true. You need to put yourself first before you can effectively help others. This is not selfishness—it's self-love. I do still experience my inner destructive critic creeping in at times, especially when putting my needs first. When I catch myself being negative, I take a breath and repeat the steps I've mentioned above. By the time I am finished, I am more self-aware, motivated, and ready to face new challenges. After repeating this exercise for months while being kind to myself, I learned how to love myself, trust my decisions, and recognize that I don't need approval from the outside world.

Learn About Your Critic

The sixth exercise entails discovering the role of your self-critic. It can also help you with step one of the fifth exercise where you identify what your inner critic's job is, how it fulfills that role, and how effective it is at fulfilling it.

Step one: List your critic's main responsibilities. For example, to protect you, help you avoid suffering, motivate you, discipline you, and help you grow. You'll notice that all the roles are positive in that they aim to lead you to a happier, healthier, more accomplished place. You can also think about the goals that your critic is pushing you toward. What achievements does it aim for? What values is it trying to live up to?

Step two: Write down the tasks that your self-critic does to fulfill its roles. For example, does your critic procrastinate, judge, scold, or support? Does it make you feel guilty for resting and devoting time to other areas of your life? Pay attention to how your body reacts to these realizations.

Step three: List your critic's successes and the cost of these achievements. Ask yourself, has your critic been successful and effective in its roles? Have you succeeded because of its negativity or despite it?

This exercise can help you evaluate your self-critic and if it's not effectively helping you achieve your goals, try to tweak its tasks and roles to be more self-reflective and self-compassionate.

Body Scan Meditation

This exercise involves connecting with your body and aims to increase your mindfulness. The goal is to systematically focus on different parts of your body and its sensations.

Step one: Get ready. Sit in a comfortable position on the floor or in a chair and focus on your breathing. As you breathe in and out, prepare your mind to focus and close your eyes. Make sure you aren't too comfortable so that you don't fall asleep. You must stay present in your body and alert.

Step two: Target your focus. Slowly and deliberately, bring your attention to the top of your head. Without moving or touching, focus on the surface of your skin. Try to expand your awareness across the surface area of your head. Try to sense your scalp, eyelids, ears, and nose. Then, move your attention across your face, down your neck, across your shoulders, down your back, and all the way down to your toes. As you move your awareness to each body part, try to discover new sensations. For example, the feeling of the ground below you, your clothes, the temperature of the room, any slight movements, or the weight distributed across your body as you sit. Some sensations may be unpleasant, such as itchiness or soreness, but don't react to or label these sensations. Simply note the sensations and move on. If you need to move to relieve some pain, please do so.

This meditation will sharpen your concentration, still your mind, place you firmly in the moment, and prevent you from judging. You can do this exercise anywhere— from your bedroom to your office to your car. You do not necessarily need to be sitting down either. Wherever you are, if you suddenly feel the need to be mindful, just take a few moments to scan your body. It won't be as effective as when you're taking time to practice it in a place free of distractions, but the exercise will help you relax and be present in your body.

This chapter has given your specific exercises to help you with the "L" part of the LOVE system: luring the voice in your head toward self-compassion. Each exercise should help you replace your negative self-criticism with self-compassion and self-reflection. In the next chapter, you will be guided through exercises to teach you to obsess over loving and accepting yourself.

CHAPTER 6

OBSESS OVER LOVING AND ACCEPTING YOURSELF

The concept of self-love is an easy one to repeat but it's not so easy to put into action. You may have mental blocks such as childhood trauma and genetics that make it significantly harder for you to love yourself. While some people can readily recognize their love for themselves without any shame or guilt, others may struggle as they fundamentally don't like themselves or mistake self-love for arrogance or narcissism. Some people want to love themselves but they don't know how to. No matter your circumstances or predispositions, as long as you choose to practice self-love, you will be able to achieve it through consistent compassion and self-acceptance. The "O" of the Love system guides you to self-love through strengthening your relationships with others and yourself so you can obsess over loving and accepting yourself.

Loving and Accepting Yourself Through Others

When we struggle to love ourselves, it's helpful to remember that loving yourself is inherently related to the people around you. When someone denies that they have any strengths, others may disagree and help them to discover and appreciate their positive traits. This is why self-love is reliant on those around you. If your friends and family express care and compassion toward your flaws and weaknesses, it softens your inner critic and reminds you that others do accept the part of you that you don't. This then suggests to you that you can and should also love the unlovable parts of yourself. In this way, your relationships with others (if they're positive and supportive) can increase your self-love.

For your close relationships to benefit you like this, you will need to make yourself vulnerable first. You must allow others to see your imperfections to give them the chance to offer their care and compassion. Only with this risk of vulnerability will you be able to forge greater intimacy with others, open yourself up to the care and love of others, and thus find authentic love for yourself. Sometimes you may indeed make yourself vulnerable and simply get hurt, but other times, you will be met with the love and support that you deeply desire. The painful encounters may cause you suffering for a while, but the worthwhile encounters will forge connections that last a lifetime. It's worth it to be vulnerable with others but be careful to whom you open up. When in doubt, trust your instincts and let others prove their worthiness over time. By being optimistic but cautious, you will allow yourself time to assess their character and values before making yourself vulnerable and save yourself from unnecessary pain.

One reason why it's so worth it to be vulnerable with others and forge true connections with people is that you get to live your true self. If you're always wearing a mask and hiding your true self, your happiness, self-love, and energy levels will be severely compromised. When you're engaged in authentic, supportive, and loving relationships, you will be surrounded by people who accept you for you. This will tell you that your true self is someone that is loved and who is worthy of that love.

If you have trouble locating your true self, ask yourself if you had to hide any part of yourself while you were growing up. Maybe you were scolded for your hobbies or personality traits or maybe others even ridiculed you for them. Receiving negative feedback on a part of your identity may have caused you to try to suppress it as a child in order to fit in and avoid rejection. This may have become an unconscious habit, so you may be stifling that part of yourself even as an adult.

Ask yourself if you feel confined or suppressed in any of your current relationships. Do any of your relationships require you to not express a certain trait or desire? Are there specific things that you don't say or do to please family and friends? You may notice that the things that you're most passionate about or the most skilled at are the things you're led to suppress; however, in supportive and loving relationships, you will not be led to suppress any part of yourself. Instead, you will be encouraged to unlock your full potential, embrace your passions, and explore your gifts. To access such relationships, you need to make space for these loving people and be vulnerable with others.

Once you locate your authentic self, think about whether the relationships you currently have either support or reject this self. Which of your friends, family members, or loved ones make you feel supported, safe, cared for, and accepted? Which of them encourages you to pursue your passions or praise your talents? Which of them provide you constructive criticism and sincerely want to see you succeed?

Alternatively, which of your loved ones makes you feel demotivated, scared, isolated, rejected, and neglected? Which of them laugh at your dreams or minimize your achievements? Which of them give you destructive criticism, push you beyond your limits, or don't respect your boundaries? Identify the people in your life who are supportive and those that are not. Try your best to leave your toxic relationships and focus more on your positive, healthy relationships. Cherish your healthy, supportive relationships, lean on them for comfort, thank them for their presence in your life, and help them when they ask for it. By focusing on these relationships, you will open yourself up to feeling the compassion of others and train yourself to be compassionate toward yourself.

Loving and Accepting Yourself on Your Own

Other than relying on your relationships with others to help you learn self-love, you can also cultivate self-love on your own. There are six steps to achieving this and it will require a lot of self-reflection and self-awareness. As you work through the steps, be patient with yourself. Remember that this journey will be tiring and emotionally draining, but the results are well worth the effort. Also, remember to reward yourself every now and then for doing the work to improve yourself. Now, let's begin!

Acceptance and Accountability

For this first step, you must be willing to feel emotional distress and take responsibility for your emotions. You must understand that everything you feel is a message that your mind or body is sending to you about your physical and mental state. This step aims to have you accept whatever you're feeling without judgment.

Simply observe your emotions and try to figure out what they're trying to tell you. Something that can help you in this step is the body scan meditation exercise provided in the previous chapter. This body scan meditation exercise will eliminate distractions, focus your mind, and reduce your judgments so that you can more calmly assess those emotions. You can also use other compassion exercises for this step to open yourself up to compassion while you're acknowledging, accepting, and confronting your negative emotions.

Overall, this first step wants you to move toward your feelings (especially the painful and negative ones that you may usually run away from) rather than away from them. You must accept responsibility for your feelings—you can't control them and they're neither morally good nor bad. What you do control is how you choose to respond to your emotions. Once you accept what you're feeling without judgment and accept responsibility for your emotions, you will be more able to approach your emotions and handle them rationally. Some things to avoid as you perform this step are self-isolation (where you get too absorbed in your own suffering), destructive criticism, substance abuse, denial, or blaming others for your emotions.

Being Open to Learning

In this second step, you must cultivate your intention to learn. As you confront negative emotions, you will probably have one of two reactions: You either will want to protect yourself from pain and deny responsibility for your emotions or circumstances, or you will want to learn about what you're doing that may be causing this emotional distress. The first option is usually the default as people don't want to be confronted with their issues. It's painful and uncomfortable, so they may resort to harmful behaviors such as addiction or avoidance. It takes more conscious effort to choose the second option and that's what this step persuades you to do. This entire step is about a single choice. Simply choose to want to learn more about your negative thoughts and actions so that you can take more loving action toward yourself. This choice is a big step toward loving yourself.

Recognize Your False Beliefs

Everyone picks up a variety of false beliefs, stigmas, wrong assumptions, and biases as they go through life. Some of these may be obvious while others may be more subconscious and subtle. Often, your false beliefs will be a significant roadblock on your path to self-love, so you must identify your false beliefs as you're starting on this journey of self-improvement. This step involves a lot of self-reflection. You will need to probe your inner self, investigate your core values and beliefs, discover how your various beliefs play into your life, and figure out which beliefs are causing you pain. As you do all this you must remember to be compassionate toward yourself. During your self-reflection, if you feel yourself starting to be too negative or destructively critical, try to practice some of the compassion exercises provided in the previous chapter. One tip to help you in this self-reflection is to ask yourself what thoughts or actions are causing you to feel anxious, depressed, guilty, jealous, angry, lonely, empty, or shameful. You can try to use mindfulness to allow your true self to answer. Once you have your answer, try to explore what fears or false beliefs may have led you to the thoughts and actions that are hurting you. Identifying your false beliefs is important as it allows you to challenge the thoughts that are preventing you from loving yourself.

Talking to Your Higher Self

This step may sound very abstract but your lower self is the unproductive, negative, unhelpful side of you while your higher self is your helpful, compassionate, loving, and wise side that can help you realistically pursue your goals and be content in your life. A key way to access this higher self is to open yourself up to self-love and self-compassion. You don't have to master it, but just being open to these concepts will make you more likely to access your higher self. Then, through self-reflection, meditation, and other practices of self-compassion, your higher self will be able to guide you to apply love and kindness to yourself. The clearer and louder your higher self becomes, the better it can tell you what to do to help yourself. Ask your higher self to reassess and improve your negative voice, your actions, and habits. This process can take a few minutes, days, weeks, or even months. Eventually, you will make important connections, receive more insights about yourself, and be able to make more productive plans to tackle the problems that you're facing.

Loving Action

For this step, you must take the insights you gained in step four and turn them into positive actions. One common loving action is to tend to your own needs. Often, step four may lead you to discover that you're sad, angry, or stressed because you're not taking care of yourself. The positive action you can take to tend to this issue is to remember to put yourself first. Another common insight that people gain is that they often believe that others see the worst in them (whether this is based on logic or not). The loving action you can take in response to this is to stop yourself from spiraling when you think this, remind yourself that you can't know the thoughts of others, and tell yourself that assuming the worst is always unhelpful. Loving actions should make you feel loved and cared for, and provide you with tangible ways of showing yourself some much-needed love.

Evaluation

After you've done the five steps to promote your self-love, remember to be mindful and check in on yourself. Has your loving action helped shake off some of your emotional distress? Do you feel more compassionate toward yourself? If you don't find the answers you're hoping for, don't lose motivation— self-love is a long and hard process. What's important is not how fast you progress but that you keep working hard. And remember, being patient with yourself is part of self-love.

Repeat these six steps as many times as you need until you reach your goals. In the end, you will find more peace, joy, and self-worth than you had before.

In the next chapter, you will learn about the fourth step in the LOVE system: viewing others through the eyes of love and compassion.

CHAPTER 7

VIEW OTHERS THROUGH THE EYES OF LOVE AND COMPASSION

Loving yourself means that you will have more love available for everyone close to you. You will be more content, self-aware, and happy, and these emotions will manifest in your relationships. Still, it's important for you to consciously work on your relationships with others. Even as you improve your relationship with yourself, you must remember that your relationships and connections are the support system and sources of love (to give and to receive) in your life. You should never take others for granted, so in this chapter, you will learn about how you can treat others better.

Your self-love and your love for others act upon each other. When one increases, so does the other. This is because you may like yourself more when you see that you're able to contribute to the lives of others. You may also feel more compassion and love for yourself when you notice how you've built reciprocal and mutually beneficial relationships. The increased love and support you will get from the relationships which you pour love into will also increase your sense of self-love as you observe how deeply others care for you.

Luckily, loving others is usually not as confounding or difficult as loving yourself. Many people find it easy to love others but they're met with a lot of resistance when they try to love themselves; however, there are still proper ways to love others. While trying to care for others, you may accidentally become overbearing, overly critical, neglect yourself too much, have ulterior motives that you may not realize, or become too demanding. As willing as you are to give love to others, it can still be a challenging task to offer your love productively and compassionately if you don't know the proper and healthy ways to do so.

One useful thing that you can do is to take all the advice you've received so far on loving yourself and apply it to your loved ones. In this chapter, you will study four main methods of loving others: showing your appreciation to others, interacting with others, displaying integrity, and forgiving others for their past mistakes.

These four methods can play into each other so, by practicing one method, you may increase your abilities in another method. That being said, you can try to focus on one or two methods first. Pick the ones that relate most to you. After you can comfortably practice these two methods, you can try to cultivate the other two. Whichever methods you choose to focus on, you will increase your ability to productively and effectively offer your love to others.

Appreciating Others

This can be shown through your actions, choices, and words. For example, you can show your appreciation of others by prioritizing them and spending more quality time with them. You can also use supportive and affirming words to talk to them and show them that you accept and love them for who they are. Remember that just as you benefit from feeling accepted unconditionally, they will also receive positive effects from your approval and acceptance. Doing this will develop your ability to show love and empathy to others and train you to cultivate self-love. The more you practice showing love to others, the easier it will be to show love to yourself.

Appreciating others also entails compassion. Even when others disappoint you or fail, you will be able to be supportive and loving by noting and praising their efforts. This will help make you a less critical person and train you to look on the positive side of things. Again, this will help you develop your self-love as you will get used to practicing compassion on others and thus be more inclined not to judge yourself too harshly. Aside from the examples listed previously, appreciating others entails:

- making a conscious effort to spend time with them to do mutually enjoyable activities.

- valuing others for their actions, words, and intentions. You can notice the small things that they do and feel grateful that they do them.

- accepting others just as they are. You don't judge them or overly criticize them. When you do offer your criticisms and opinions, they are always constructive and considerate.

- being able to overlook their small, harmless mistakes. You don't obsess or hold onto the small things they do that may annoy you momentarily. You can let things go. If there is a serious issue, you can approach them and have a productive conversation about what is bothering you.

Interacting With Others

This step involves deepening your bonds with others while investing time and energy into social support. All this will bring you feelings of empathy, productivity, connectedness, and happiness. Through your interactions with others, you can learn more about them (as you have conversations and observe them), discover insights about yourself (as you observe how you interact with others and react to certain situations), and realize new and different perspectives (as you try to see things from their point of view). You will also be able to offer your loved ones a shoulder to cry on or a sympathetic ear. Being confided in and trusted will increase your self-esteem and increase your empathy. In turn, you will have a network of loved ones ready to offer you their support and advice. This may lead you to gain newfound wisdom and more realistic perspectives on your situations. Some components of interacting with others are:

- being open and receptive to receiving love, kindness, and affection from others. For example, being able to receive compliments, gifts, or physical gestures of love.

- using words and actions to show your love to others. You must be comfortable verbalizing your affections and conveying them to others. You must also be willing to show others how you feel. This will make them more comfortable and willing to demonstrate their love to you in return.

- providing others with the support that they need, whether it's emotional or practical support. You will set aside the time to help your loved ones. You will stay by their side even if you're not doing anything to practical help (often, your presence will be enough to soothe and help them). You will volunteer to help them with big or small tasks.

- keeping things interesting. Healthy relationships last for a long time and in that time, things may become boring or routine, so try keeping things interesting. Add some elements of fun and surprise into your relationships such as trying new restaurants or hobbies. This will show others that you're putting in the effort to improve the relationship.

- being there for others through thick and thin. No matter what they're going through, you must be there for your loved ones. Whether they're experiencing a bad breakup or a promotion at work, you will be there to comfort or congratulate them.

Integrity

Integrity entails honesty and moral uprightness (simply doing what you think is right). If you show integrity in a relationship, you can increase the trust between both parties. Here are some examples of behaviors that display integrity.

- Telling the truth to your loved ones even if it's not advantageous for you. Even if the truth paints you in a bad light, you don't try to lie or con your way out of the discussion. Avoiding talking about it does not show integrity as you are keeping the truth from them.

- Respecting your commitments and upholding your promises. Sometimes you may make promises or commitments that you later want to back out of because it's inconvenient for you. A person with integrity would honor their word and keep their promises. By not going back on your commitments and promises, you teach others that they can trust you and rely on you.

- Being honest with yourself and abiding by your values. Someone with integrity will live life by their personal beliefs and values. They will allow their moral compass to direct them and guide their actions and choices. To know your values, you must first be honest with yourself and reflect.

Forgiveness

Finally, the fourth component of loving others is forgiving them for past hurts. Healthy relationships will last for a long time and both parties will inevitably injure each other. Healthy relationships involve both parties seeking forgiveness. When you seek forgiveness, you will increase your humility, empathy, and understanding. When you choose to forgive, you will increase your compassion, love, and kindness. This will also increase your ability to love yourself. When you practice forgiveness on others, you will be more able to practice forgiveness on yourself. Forgiving others involves:

- being able to forgive yourself for your own mistakes and imperfections. If you can't forgive yourself, you will find it more difficult to forgive others as your mind will be attuned to holding grudges and being critical.

- showing and expressing your emotions. If someone has hurt you, you will be able to communicate with them and inform them of how their words or actions have affected you negatively.

- releasing your past hurt whether or not the person who hurt you regrets it or apologizes. Most of the time, forgiveness has more to do with you than with the other person. Even if the person who hurt you doesn't feel bad about it or doesn't think they did anything wrong, you should still forgive as this releases you from unnecessary suffering. If you keep holding onto a grudge, you will only bring your past pain into your present. When you release your past pain, you free yourself.

- not keeping score. This means that you're able to let small things go. You are not calculative and you don't hold every mistake someone makes against them.

Now that you've learned how to view others through the eyes of love and compassion, let's move on to the last step of the LOVE system and learn how to embrace the world around you.

CHAPTER 8

EMBRACE THE WORLD

L ove can sustain and increase itself, spreading out to touch all aspects of your life. In the last chapter, you discovered how your self-love can affect and is affected by your love for others. When you love yourself, you'll find that you are happier and possess more love to share. When you love others, you practice loving yourself and improving your self-image.

Your self-love may also lead you to interact with the world around you through the eyes of love. When you have more self-love, you will be more positive and open to new experiences which may change how you view and act in the world. You will begin to view things not through the eyes of pessimism or cynicism but through the eyes of love. As you're walking on the path to self-love, you should be trying to lovingly embrace the world as this will enable you to love yourself more. As you train yourself to love and embrace the world, you may become a generally more accepting person and this may help you to accept yourself and be more compassionate toward yourself.

The Five Components of Love

Now you will learn the five components of loving the world that you can consciously practice. These five components are love as patience, love as kindness, love as delight in the success of others, love as humility, and love as empathy. These elements may already have been developed in you as you strive to increase your self-love. Either way, it's beneficial for you to be aware of these components so that you can love the world more easily and readily.

Love as Patience

Whenever you want to show others how much you love them or whenever you want to live your life as an expression of love, remember that a big part of love is patience. Don't get distracted by perfectionism in your life—this will only make you impatient. Perfectionism provides you with skewed and unrealistic expectations of everything, and when things in your life don't live up to these expectations, you may become irritated. This will lead you to mistreat people and mishandle unexpected challenges. Perfectionism and expecting everything to be up to your personal standards will only lower your quality of life. Rather than perfectionism, try to practice patience in your life. This will help you enjoy the journey of life without rushing through it.

While perfectionism solely emphasizes the results and makes you shortsighted by ignoring the journey of getting there, patience expands your perspective, helps you appreciate the nuances of life, and gives you time to savor more of life. This can not only increase the quality of your life and your relationships, it can even make you more mindful, grounded, and present in your own life. Being more focused and less caught up in the result allows you to really experience life. Your relationships will be improved as you will be more understanding and compassionate to others. This will attract others to you and make them more grateful for you. You will also be more mindful and present as you won't be living in a projected future.

Love as Kindness

Kind and loving actions are monumentally powerful and influential. A small, seemingly insignificant act of kindness can be a turning point in someone else's life and be remembered for years to come. You never know how your kind acts may affect others or influence the world, but it's a good enough feeling to keep doing kind acts and hoping that others can benefit from you. This can make you feel like you're contributing to the world. If anything, the posi-

tive emotions you get from doing kind deeds will help you
see the world in a more positive, optimistic light. Even if
you don't see the immediate effects of your kindness, you
can rest assured that anyone you are kind to feels a positive
difference.

Kindness can be like water as it can lubricate the tensions
in a relationship, soothe others during times of trouble,
and smooth over the rough edges of the most disagreeable
people. If there has been a recent conflict within a relationship or if there's someone that you simply don't like, kindness can be like an olive branch that offers love as a bridge
to each other. If you know people who are struggling and
going through dark times, kindness can be a light that offers them hope, solidarity, sympathy, and understanding.
Your kindness can lighten the burden they feel for a while
as they're reminded of the good that still exists in the world
amidst all the bad. If you encounter someone who's simply
grouchy and who has a permanent foul mood, kindness
can be used to combat their attitude. Eventually, your positive attitude may outshine their negative one and put them
in a better mood. It's always nicer to be treated kindly than
unkindly. This may not always work but that doesn't mean
that you should stop being kind to such people. Don't let
others influence how you act. You influence how they act.
Be true to yourself and keep being kind. This is in line with
your journey to self-love and self-improvement.

When you avoid your primal urge to be rude, angry, or
disrespectful and instead choose to interact with the world

through love and kindness, your life will be filled with positivity, connectedness, and gratitude.

Love as Rejoicing in the Success of Others

Other than kindness, interacting with the world through the eyes of love entails rejoicing in the success of others. Many people view life as a race or a competition and they interact with the world as if it were them against all else. If others have something, they view it as something that was taken from them. If others win or achieve something, they view it as a loss for themselves and a sign of their own inadequacy. If others have a positive personality trait, they view it as something that they must also have to measure up to and be better than others. This method of interacting with the world is highly negative, not to mention exhausting. You will always be chasing opportunities, feeling inadequate, and opening yourself up to envy, loss, self-pity, self-loathing, greed, and inadequacy. Coveting what others have and resenting their success will make you a bitter person and an unsupportive friend; however, if you choose to interact with the world through the eyes of love, you will be able to view life not as a competition but as a trek or a quest that you are taking with other people. You're not in competition with others—you're all helping each other reach new heights on this shared journey. Once you view life like this, you'll be able to rejoice in the success of others. Their good news will not mean bad news for you, so you will be able to view their good news as wholly positive. This will make you a more sincere and supportive person. Consequently, your relationships will be improved and your quality of life will be enhanced. Viewing life as a shared journey will also increase your empathy as you will be able to share in the successes of others as well as their failures and willingly offer your support and encouragement in both instances.

If you're having trouble with this component of love, try to spend some time in self-reflection to develop your sense of self, understand what makes you unique, and determine your core values. Having more self-awareness will increase your compassion and your ability to be genuinely happy for others.

Love as Humility

To better understand this concept, let's explore its opposite: arrogance. Arrogance can come from two sources: You may truly believe in your inflated sense of worth or you may be using arrogance as a shield to hide low self-esteem. Both sources of arrogance may express themselves in the same way. You may overemphasize your achievements, ridicule the achievements of others, criticize others, and close yourself off from the opinions of others. This will negatively impact the quality of your relationships and taint how you view and interact with the world. You will also open yourself up to more negative emotions.

If you are arrogant and you truly believe in your inflated sense of worth, you may experience disillusionment and denial when reality shows you that you're not as great as you think you are. If you are arrogant to bolster and protect your low sense of worth, you may feel good about yourself for a moment but then you will feel worse later on. In the moment, when you're putting others down to feel better about yourself, you're inflating your sense of worth; however, you will feel worse about yourself when comparing yourself with others whom you deem better than you. There will always seem like there's someone who's got it better than you. Rather than practicing arrogance which will only lower your quality of life and make you more vulnerable to low self-worth, humility can help you see yourself more favorably.

With humility, you can accept your failures and mistakes, you don't base your worth on others through comparison, and you assign equal value to everyone by seeing their intrinsic worth. When you can admit your flaws and imperfections, you can have a realistic view of yourself and work to improve yourself. This can improve your self-worth. When you stop basing your worth on others, you will stop feeling the need to tear others down and channel that energy into being a more supportive friend. When you treat everyone based on their inherent worth, you will be a more respectful and grounded person which will in turn improve your relationships.

Love as Empathy

Finally, to embrace the world is to view love as empathy. This is an important component of love as to truly love someone else, you must be able to understand them and put yourself in their shoes. This way, you can appreciate what they're going through and what has made them the way they are now. To practice empathy, you must make a constant and conscious effort to understand others, no matter what they're going through, whether or not you approve of their actions, and whether or not you know all the details. When you try to understand others, you will be able to see things from different perspectives and feel a deeper love for others.

Being Open to Exploration

Other than cultivating the five components of love that will help you embrace the world, there are a million other things you can do. These possibilities will open themselves to you when you prove that you are open to exploring the world. In this section, you will learn how to do so and also receive suggestions on what to explore.

Understand Your Comfort Zone

For you to break out of your comfort zone, you first need to understand where that zone is and where it originates. Your comfort zone may have been developed from childhood experiences and evolved through subsequent fears and worries. For example, you may have been told that you aren't any good at sports as a child, so now you stay away from physical activity. Or you may worry a lot about money as an adult and so you avoid traveling. Once you're able to identify your comfort zone, you will be able to analyze and assess whether it is a real limitation or a self-created one. This will put you in the position to take action and overcome any fears that are stopping you from trying new things.

Take It Slow and Practice

If you want to exercise more, don't immediately join a competitive sports team. This will only place you under unnecessary stress and demand more than you're able to give at the moment. Instead, join a recreation club or a sports team that plays for fun. This will push you to improve your skills and provide you with new experiences. You will gain a nurturing environment that will harness your abilities rather than a competitive and intense environment that may pressure or demotivate you. Remember, you can't be the best when you're just starting something new and challenging. Don't approach your new experiences as an assessment of your skills or value. Instead, try to see them as fun avenues of learning. You must be willing to be a beginner and an amateur if you want to explore and embrace life. If you only try activities that you know you're already good at, you limit your experiences and opportunities for learning.

If you're hesitant to explore, remind yourself that it's good for you. The areas in your brain that activate when you're happy and when you learn new things are closely related. When you're learning something new and interesting, your happiness and contentment will increase. This can help you with the next method of exploration which is practice. The more you practice, the easier things will become. You will slowly improve at your new activity and exploring new skills won't seem so daunting anymore.

Stay Curious

Another good way to approach exploring life is to let your curiosity guide you. Don't feel like you should be interested in hobbies that are useful or profitable—simply let yourself be interested in whatever genuinely attracts you and then do it. By trusting your desires, you are showing yourself that your happiness is worth the time and effort it takes to learn something new. Maybe there is a niche sport that you've always been interested in but never dared to try. Maybe it's a recent trend that you haven't had the time to pursue yet. Whatever it is, let your curiosity and interests lead you to your next new activity and embrace your new self-knowledge.

Overcoming Fear

One reason you may have procrastinated on pursuing your curiosities or interests is fear, so the last tip on exploring life is to put your anxieties in perspective. Some fears and worries are real while others are imagined. If you're feeling anxious about trying something new, try to take a step back and view the experience objectively. Is your fear reasonable or irrational? Consider the worst that could happen and if serious physical harm is a real probability, then take steps to prevent it and ensure that an instructor is present. If the only danger is failure, then push yourself to try it anyway. Even if you fail, you'll have gained a new experience and allowed yourself to learn from it. This can also be a good opportunity for you to practice self-compassion.

As for what you can explore, the possibilities are endless! Other than simply pursuing whatever your curiosity pulls you toward, you can also explore nature, your hometown, and the lives around you. The internet will be a useful tool for you as you can search for any information or instructions for almost anything. You can also look for online classes in your area of interest. Alternatively, if someone inspires you to try a new hobby, you can ask them to teach you or you can look for local classes involved in the specific activity. To explore nature, you can go on walks or hikes or join an outdoor sports team. If you want to invest more time and also get a good workout, you can build a garden in your backyard. This will take a lot of work but you will definitely get more connected with nature. If it's too much work and space to create your own garden, you can always offer to help a friend with their garden. They will appreciate the help and you'll get to spend more time tending to nature and your friendship.

There are also ways to explore your hometown. If you've lived in the same place for a long time, you may think that there's nothing new to explore. This is a limiting and false belief as there is always something new to discover no matter where you are. One way you can discover more things is to go to your local community center. They may have interesting new activities or classes that you can get involved in. Or you can ask your family and friends where their favorite places to eat or hang out are. You can even try going on a tour of your town. You may usually avoid tourist spots, but try to be open to them this time. You may enjoy it and even if you don't, at least you tried it.

Finally, to explore the lives around you, you can try doing community work or volunteering. This will expose you to the lives of other people with whom you may never have interacted otherwise. You may meet interesting people, increase your empathy, and expand your worldview. Other than this, you can also try to invest more time in your current relationships with your family members, a close friend, or a new acquaintance. Whomever it is, try to spend more time with them and show a genuine interest in their life. This may lead you to forge deeper connections with others and discover new things about their lives.

Being open to exploring the world is an undeniably beneficial trait to have. You will not only open yourself up to new experiences, but you will also make your life more meaningful, engaging, and interesting. You will even open yourself up to more love—loving others, yourself, and the world. Love is not something that simply happens. It requires effort and time. You must continuously develop and maintain it. You must also make several conscious decisions to be open to the world around you.

In the end, the products of your hard work will be healthier relationships, a happier life, more engaging days, and a more positive outlook on the world. Remember to express your love regularly and authentically to yourself, others, and the world around you.

CONCLUSION: LIVING TO LOVE AND LOVING TO LIVE

As you've reached the end of this book, I hope that you feel more empowered than when you started. I especially hope you feel a greater sense of self-love and self-compassion. Even if you don't, there's no need to worry. Such skills are a struggle to obtain and it may take you a long time and countless hours to cultivate them in your life. For now, it's enough to simply feel more equipped and willing to work to increase your self-love and self-compassion.

Through the course of this book, I have emphasized that self-love is a worthy goal that will improve your relationships with yourself, with others, and with the world around you. You also gained a wealth of practical and theoretical information that will act as both the map and the tools that you'll need on your journey to self-love and self-improvement.

Before you close this book, let's quickly review all the things that you've learned to help you retain the information and give you a closing guide on which chapters to revisit if you want to review some information.

In Chapter 1, you learned about your inner critic and the two vastly different methods of criticizing yourself: destructive criticism and constructive criticism. You studied the characteristics and effects of both to understand why and how destructive criticism is an unproductive, unhelpful waste of your time and energy while constructive criticism is well worth your time.

In Chapter 2, you explored self-compassion which can unlock and unleash your self-love. You studied the various and extensive benefits of self-compassion to show yourself that it's a necessary and positive attribute to cultivate. You also revised the three components of self-compassion: self-kindness, mindfulness, and common humanity. Self-kindness is your ability to treat yourself as you would treat a good friend. Mindfulness is your ability to be present in the moment. Common humanity is your ability to relate yourself to the universal human experience. All these things will help you be more compassionate toward yourself.

In Chapter 3, you noted the three masks of self-compassion so that you don't fall into the trap of mistaking them for self-compassion. This would result in detrimental effects on your mental health and general happiness. The three masks of self-compassion are self-pity, self-indulgence, and self-esteem. The first two masks are always harmful whereas self-esteem is a positive concept that is only harmful when mistaken for self-compassion.

In Chapter 4, you learned about self-reflection and how it differs from negative self-criticism. While destructive criticism is unhelpful and unproductive, self-reflection can offer you insights and a balanced perspective. This was underscored to you along with various other benefits of self-reflection. At the end of this chapter, you received practical advice on how to switch from self-criticism to self-reflection.

In Chapter 5, you received practical advice on how to execute the second step in the LOVE system: luring your inner critic toward self-compassion. You were also led through various exercises to increase your self-compassion.

In Chapter 6, you moved on to the third step in the LOVE system: obsessing over loving and accepting yourself. You were advised on how to do this through your relationships with others and on your own.

In Chapter 7, you landed on the fourth step in the LOVE system: viewing others through the eyes of love. You were guided through concepts of appreciation, interaction, integrity, and forgiveness. Developing these traits should help you to be a more loving person overall.

Finally, in Chapter 8, you were taught the fifth step in the LOVE system: embracing the world. Through patience, kindness, joy for the success of others, humility, and empathy, you learned how to change how you view and interact with the world to increase your quality of life and general happiness.

A Message From the Author

I truly believe that the information provided in this book can change your life. I can't begin to tell you how much it helped me. Thinking back, I used to feel lost and helpless. My life was great on paper but my internal life and headspace were dreadful. I was being consumed by my destructive criticism and unfair expectations of myself. Anytime I tried to address the issues that were making me feel bad about myself, it would just result in an unproductive session of self-loathing, blame, and guilt. I'm sure that many women can relate to those feelings of inadequacy, pressure, and self-judgment that I was going through. I'm sure that many women can understand how your thoughts can tear you apart and create visceral reactions of fear, stress, and sadness. It's a dark and lonely feeling. Thankfully, as I reflect on that period of my life now, I don't judge myself for having experienced those emotions or for having been trapped in certain habits. The self-love and self-compassion that I have built up allow me to look back on the hard times and feel grateful rather than judgmental. I'm grateful for having gone through what I did as I can see it as part of my life's journey, as part of what has shaped me, and as part of my current understanding of the world. I'm even more grateful for what I've learned as a result which I'm now able to share with other women experiencing the same issues.

Honestly, as I was learning all the practical and theoretical information contained in this book, I was overwhelmed and frustrated. Luckily, the theoretical knowledge helped me remain motivated. I knew what I was doing wrong and how those errors were costing me, so I was more determined than ever to improve and stop self-sabotaging. The practical knowledge then came to my aid as I had clear steps I could follow to achieve my goals. The steps were easy to understand but that didn't make them easy to execute. I had to constantly remind myself to be patient. Every failure or setback became another opportunity for me to practice my self-love and self-compassion. It was an arduous journey but every nugget of information was like an extra tool that I could use against my destructive habits and thoughts. I slowly collected more and more tools, and eventually, the battle against my destructive criticism got easier.

Now, I consider all the knowledge I gathered along the way as my invaluable treasures. I know exactly where I would be without them and for that reason, I am eternally grateful that I took the time to practice each skill. Even as my life started to improve, I kept each lesson fresh in my mind by journaling and tracking my progress. Another great thing about this knowledge is that no one can take it away from me. Practicing self-love and self-compassion has become a habit and it's within my power to offer it to others. Now that this information is in your possession, I hope you put it into practice and thrive.

All the information that you have gained so far is aimed at increasing your love for yourself, others, and the world. When you live with love as a priority, you will enjoy the world more, experience life more intensely, gain more meaningful relationships, and feel more at peace with yourself. In other words, when you live to love, you will love to live. With this, I hope you close this book with the conviction and motivation to make loving changes in your life. Be patient and refer back to each step as many times as needed until you master the art of self-love. Self-love is the greatest gift you can offer yourself in this lifetime and you deserve it. As long as you have the intention and the will, you can do anything!

REFERENCES

Ackerman, C. (2017, December 21). *9 Self-compassion exercises & worksheets for increasing compassion.* PositivePsychology.com. https://positivepsychology.com/self-compassion-exercises-worksheets/

Black, C. (2020, February 11). *The pros and cons of being self-critical (and how to strike a balance).* Lifehack. https://www.lifehack.org/863533/self-critical

Bleidorn, W., Arslan, R. C., Jaap J. A. Denissen, Rentfrow, P. J., Gebauer, J. E., Potter, J., & Gosling, S. D. (2016). Age and gender differences in self-esteem—A cross-cultural window. *Journal of Personality and Social Psychology, 111*(3), 396–410. https://doi.org/10.1037/pspp0000078

Chambers, R., Lo, B. C. Y., & Allen, N. B. (2008). The impact of intensive mindfulness training on attentional control, cognitive style, and affect. *Cognitive therapy and research, 32*(3), 303–322. https://doi.org/10.1007/s10608-007-9119-0

Cherry, K. (2021, July 20). *What exactly is self-esteem?* Verywell Mind. https://www.verywellmind.com/what-is-self-esteem-2795868

Davis, D. M., & Hayes, J. A. (2012). *What are the benefits of mindfulness?* American Psychological Association. https://www.apa.org/monitor/2012/07-08/ce-corner

Engel, B. (2018, June 19). *Using the practice of self-kindness to cope with stress.* Psychology Today. https://www.psychologytoday.com/intl/blog/the-compassion-chronicles/201806/using-the-practice-self-kindness-cope-stress

Farb, N. A., Anderson, A. K., Mayberg, H., Bean, J., McKeon, D., & Segal, Z. V. (2010). Minding one's emotions: mindfulness training alters the neural expression of sadness. *Emotion, 10*(1), 25.

Firestone, L. (2016, November 1). *The many benefits of self-compassion.* PsychAlive. https://www.psychalive.org/many-benefits-of-self-compassion/

Frank Porter Graham Child Development Institiute. (2022). *What self-compassion is not.* FPG Program on Mindfulness & Self-Compassion for Families. Selfcompassion.web.unc.edu. https://selfcompassion.web.unc.edu/what-is-self-compassion/what-self-compassion-is-not/

Gilbertson, T. (2015, April 3). *The paradox of self-pity.* Psychology Today. https://www.psychologytoday.com/us/blog/constructive-wallowing/201504/the-paradox-self-pity

Golden, B. (2019, January 12). *How self-criticism threatens you in mind and body.* Psychology Today. https://www.psychologytoday.com/us/blog/overcoming-destructive-anger/201901/how-self-criticism-threatens-you-in-mind-and-body

Kelly, A. (2019, May 29). *Are you self-critical?* Psychology Today. https://www.psychologytoday.com/us/blog/all-about-attitude/201905/are-you-self-critical

Kennedy, T. (2018, April 10). *How self-reflection gives you a happier and more successful life.* Lifehack. https://www.lifehack.org/696285/how-self-reflection-gives-you-a-happier-and-more-successful-life

Lazar, S. W., Kerr, C. E., Wasserman, R. H., Gray, J. R., Greve, D. N., Treadway, M. T., and Fischl, B. (2005). Meditation experience is associated with increased cortical thickness. *Neuroreport, 16*(17), 1893.

Neff, K. (2011, April 17). *Is it self-indulgent to be self-compassionate? Self-compassion.* https://self-compassion.org/is-it-self-indulgent-to-be-self-compassionate/

Oxford English Dictionary. (n.d.). compassion, n. In *Oxford english dictionary online.* https://www.oed.com/viewdictionaryentry/Entry/37475

Schroeder, M. (2016, March 17). *Self-criticism can be psychologically devastating—how to overcome it.* US News. https://health.usnews.com/wellness/articles/2016-03-17/self-criticism-can-be-psychologically-devastating-how-to-overcome-it

Seppala, E. (2014, May 9). *The scientific benefits of self-compassion.* The Center for Compassion and Altruism Research and Education. http://ccare.stanford.edu/uncategorized/the-scientific-benefits-of-self-compassion-infographic/

Wignall, N. (2021, May 3). *4 psychological reasons you're so self-critical.* SIMPLE. https://medium.com/simple-pub/4-psychological-reasons-youre-so-self-critical-daa3494bf7a8

Made in United States
North Haven, CT
10 December 2022

28421252R00083